SCOTLAND
CASTLES AND CLANS
———— THE LEGENDS

SCOTLAND CASTLES AND CLANS
──────── THE LEGENDS

Brian C. Mack FSA Scot

Artist:
Karol K. Mack O.P.A.
Fellow of the American Artists Professional League

FRONTISPIECE: Castle Stalker (8" x 10" oil)

All rights reserved. No part of this book shall be reproduced, stored in an information retrieval system, or transmitted in any form or by any means, mechanical or electrical, photocopied or recorded, without the express written consent from the author and without full and proper written acknowledgment of the author.

Library of Congress Number (LCCN): 2009901261
ISBN: 1-4392-2826-4

Book Design: Sean Conrad
Illustrations: Karol K. Mack
Original Artwork: Karol K. Mack
All Photographs: Brian C. Mack

The information contained in SCOTLAND: CASTLES AND CLANS THE LEGENDS is believed to be accurate at the time of printing, but no representation or warranty is given (express or implied) as to its accuracy, completeness or correctness. The author shall not accept any liability whatsoever for any direct, indirect or consequential loss or damage arising in any way from any use of or reliance on this material for any purpose.

Parts of this book contain works of historical fiction. Names, characters, places and incidents can either be a product of the author's imagination or are used fictitiously. While every care has been taken to compile and check all information in this book, in a work of this complexity it is possible that mistakes and omissions have occurred. If you know of any corrections, alterations, or improvements, please contact the author through www.castlesandclans.com

Acknowledgements

My sincerest thanks to those who have helped with the preparation of this book:

Vic Anderson, Charlotte Berney, Dennis Brown, Laura Brown, Harry Chronis,
Sean Conrad, Alastair Cunningham, Dennis Mack, Karol K. Mack,
Pat McKee, Gary Miller, Steve Mitchell, Sandra L. Patterson-Slaydon,
Cydney Springer, and John Todd.

SCOTLAND: CASTLES AND CLANS THE LEGENDS
First Published in 2010
Estes Park, CO
Printed in the U.S.A.
Copyright © Brian C. Mack 2010

CONTENTS

Introduction VI

The Highlands 8
The Highlands Map 9
Recurring Dreams, Kisimul Castle 12 • Invasions, Rothesay Castle 16
The Destiny of a Nation, Scone Palace 19 • Shadows in the Wind, Huntly Castle 22
Central Locations, Castle Tioram 24 • Time Stops Here, Duart Castle 26
Alliances, Dunstaffnage Castle 29 • Sign of the Cross, Urquhart Castle 32
Lines of Sight, Eilean Donan Castle 34 • Seasons, Blair Castle 37
No Escape, Mingary Castle 40 • Intent and Desire, Dunvegan Castle 43
All Queens and No Kings, Doune Castle 46 • Always Welcome, Kilravock Castle 49
Symbols of Strength, Castle Stalker 52 • Keystones of the Realm, Kilchurn Castle 54
Partnerships, Craigievar Castle 56 • Gatherings, Braemar Castle 58

The Lowlands 64
The Lowlands Map 65
Wizards of Intuition, Threave Castle 68 • The Axis, Linlithgow Palace 74
Alternate Routes, Traquair House 78 • Boundaries, Fyvie Castle 80
Side by Side, Neidpath Castle 83 • Webs of Betrayel, Dunure Castle 87
Larger Schemes, Hume Castle 91 • Beneath the Surface, Aberdour Castle 94
Prophecies, Hermitage Castle 97 • Peasants and Maids, Dunnottar Castle 101
Unintended Consequences, Hoddom Castle 104 • Hidden Away, Glamis Castle 107
Disruptions, Tantallon Castle 111 • Below and Above, Blackness Castle 114
Signs of Life, Spynie Castle 116 • Acts of Parliament, Hallbar Tower 118
Watchful Eyes, Dunskey Castle 120 • Revealed, Culzean Castle 124

Clan Map 128
Royal Dynasties and Monarchs of Scotland 129
Glossary 130 - 132
Selected Further Reading 133
Family Name / Clan Index 134
Index 135-138

Auchinleck House, Ayrshire Scotland

Introduction

Legends: The word comes from Latin legenda, meaning things to be read.

A Scottish brogue is immediately recognizable and transforms mundane speech into a song. Accepting sound as a symbol, Scotland's voices create a great choir representing a collective memory comprised of legends. Past or present, the words that define a nation's heritage come to life through human voices.

From time immemorial stories have been handed down the world over. A legend is foremost a collection of beliefs relaying past events that exemplify the hopes, fears, and loves of a people. The Scottish tales told here are fictional, yet have a foundation in facts loosely based on characters in history, locations on maps, and recorded events.

Most legends contain insights into human character and a few examples in this book include: three young men resourceful enough to defeat an evil Redcap (assassin) and his experienced cohorts, an Earl who learns from the spiders how to weave webs, before the webs are spun around him, and a young-girl who befriends a brownie discovering the responsibilities of friendship.

My own aspirations as a story teller developed in my youth while sitting on the floor with the other children, waiting with attentive ears for words that stimulate the mind's imagination. Years later, I saw those actual locations in Scotland from the stories I heard. Forests, dark and foreboding, by their very nature lend themselves to visions of brownies, elves, and fairies. Lochs and glens are inviting settings for the tales, and encourage putting pen to paper and paint to canvas in an effort to share the enchantment with others.

Scotland's ancient writings demonstrate a verbal outpouring evidenced by their sennachies (story-tellers) who held revered positions in the clan hierarchy - the foundation of Scottish society. Continuing the tradition, modern-day wordsmiths are well versed in the histories, genealogies, and legends. Many of these stories were taken abroad as Scotland's sons and daughters populated the world. Those claiming Scottish ancestry (twenty-five million in America alone) currently outnumber the indigenous residents five to one.

I am an ancestral Scot, and October of 2008 marked a decade from my first steps on Scottish soil. During frequent visits, I am often mistaken as a Scotsman although my American accent quickly gives me away. Members of my own family left their homeland traveling to the New World over two hundred years ago, some departing from Dundee, Scotland, and others from Antrim, Northern Ireland. I am the first of my family to return, not as a citizen but a visitor, or dare I say, tourist. Throughout my initial visits to Scotland, I couldn't appreciate the landscapes and castles fully. However, after studying Karol Mack's evocative paintings, I developed a greater perspective viewing the scenes through the eyes of an artist.

As a historian I research books and interview people; whereas, the artist "interviews" the location studying color, contrast, and value. This volume is illustrated with paintings that complement the legends. The artist concentrated on the Scottish castle, an icon which fixes people to the land.

During my travels in Scotland, I was often reminded of a quotation by the Roman poet Horace. 'Quod petis, hic est, Est Ulubris animaus si te non deficit aequus.' (Whatever you seek is here, in this remote place, if only you have a good firm mind.) The words are read from the pediment above Auchenlick House (former home of James Boswell) located in the Lowlands of Scotland.

Forest near Auchinleck House

Legends themselves date back to human origins and many such as the words of Horace are older than the structures on which these quotations are engraved. The word legend first appears in the English language around the fourteenth century, a time when many castles and clans of Scotland were well-developed and recognizable in their present form.

By communicating a richer quality of what could have occurred instead of what actually did, legends are often more prevalent and lasting than proper history. For me, the retelling of the included legends was created from visiting Scotland. Its people and landscape inspired a creativity that when united with historical research, personal experiences, and interviews conjured up visions from my mind's recesses.

View from Auchinleck House

This book includes time-lines and is divided into two sections, the Highlands and Lowlands. It contains thirty-six legends that exist in history, told in story-form giving them a timeless quality. My tales possess historical traits that give the legends an element of truth, but require imagination for a complete understanding. In most instances, the stories serve to lift us above the repetitions and constraints of our daily existence transporting us into the otherworldly. They provide a bridge to the past, and if we allow them, future visions.

From the beginning of time, mere words were brought to life in oral traditions, later written, and as time passed, stored in books. Often forgotten then re-discovered in old libraries and once again read aloud, the stories developed an existence of their own. Each telling and retelling of a legend is as unique as each Scot (native or ancestral); in anthology they are a collective voice that contributes to the narrative of a nation.

Brian C. Mack
(*The introduction was first composed in Auchinleck House, 2008*)

Bridge over the Dippol Burn, Auchinleck

 # THE HIGHLANDS

Scotland, taken in its entirety, can be understood as an amalgamation of region and culture. Throughout the centuries, clans have always been more prominent to the Highlands. However, any description of indigenous Scots is based upon kinship identity. In addition to the native Scots, those of Scottish ancestry claim distinct heritage and origin.

The Highland Boundary Line should not be viewed as definitive. The Highlands or Lowlands are not official geographical regions of Scotland. There are areas of the "Highlands" that rise only a few feet above sea level such as the islands, although mountains, such as Ben Nevis, can reach up to 4,409 feet.

The Highlands as a term can be defined by cultural influences. The Celtic inhabitants of ancient Alba (Gaelic name for Scotland) were made up of diverse tribes, which in the north were comprised of Picts, Scots, and Norse. In addition to these tribes, Roman incursions into the land they called Caledonia occurred from around 71 until their exit from *Britannia* in 213. The Romans began construction of Hadrian's Wall in 122. The wall is in the southern reaches of the kingdom near the present border between Scotland and England. Further north, another Roman wall, named Antonine's Wall, was constructed twenty years later in 142. This wall spans the distance between the Firth of Clyde and the Firth of Forth.

By the 500's, the Kingdom of Dalriada (made up of Scots) existed in northwest Scotland and was believed to include Northern Ireland. The Kingdom of Scotland dates to 843 when the first Scottish King, Kenneth MacAlpine, united the Scots and the Picts. Scotland then existed as an independent state until 1707 and occupied the northern third of the island of Great Britain. Since 1482, following England's control of Berwick (a coastal town located on the border), the territory of Scotland corresponded to that of modern day geography. From 1707, the Kingdoms of Scotland and England were united to form Great Britain. This occurred under the Act of Union.

Scotland, past and present, occupies an area bounded by the North Sea to the east, the Atlantic Ocean to the north and west, and the Irish Sea to the southwest. Apart from the mainland, Scotland consists of over seven-hundred small islands.

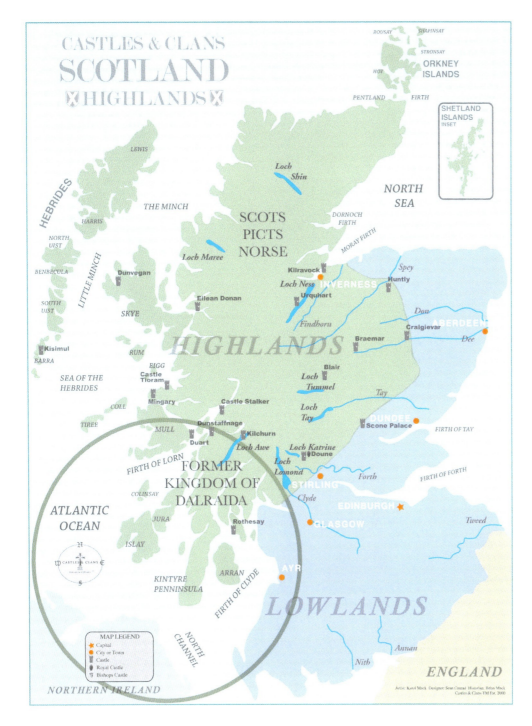

The beyond, Outside of Lossiemouth

The shores of the Moray Firth

Cairngorm Mountains

The Pass at Glencoe 24"x 36" oil

Isle of Skye 16" x 20" oil

KISIMUL CASTLE
8" X 10" oil

**Family / Clan Associations:
MacNeil, Gordon, Cathcart, and MacNeil**

Kisimul Castle is known as 'The Rock in the Bay'. The structure, an impregnable fortress with two artesian wells and a fish trap, dates to 1030. The tower rises to three-stories with a courtyard surrounded by a curtain wall. Kisimul withstood several assaults from rival clans in the fifteenth and sixteenth centuries, but it was abandoned by its owners in the nineteenth century. The castle underwent restoration in the 1930's. The painting renders Kisimul's appearance in 1998.

Recurring Dreams

A Legend of Kisimul Castle
(Told from the perspective of Connor MacNeil)

This house, once full, is now empty and void. I have come home to the Isle of Barra for a funeral, my father's – he was aged in body yet young of heart. During events such as these, I often reflect upon time. In my youth, the years seemed to pass slower than they presently proceed during adulthood. I remember once, late in the evening, discussing the issue with my father, Hamish MacNeil. He instructed, "Time is not the constant we understand it to be." Over a cup of tea he told me, "The clock in my roundhouse is a simple device. I can set the hands at any number and they, without interuption, continue on. The device lacks any past memory and is vacant of future vision." He leaned back in his chair and after a couple of puffs from his pipe, "Only the human soul is capable of measuring time or should I say, life, which can only be lived in this moment - it is the now. Unlike the clock, the hands of human existence cannot be reset."

That was the last advice he gave me. The next day, we went fishing then traveled to the pub; he greeted friend and foe alike with a smile covering his face. Soon a crowd gathered and the stories of Scotland flowed from his lips. As he spoke, my mind drifted back to what he once related: "A storyteller requires a natural happiness, an innate quality audiences recognize in the speaking of every word." He was currently telling his favorite story, *The Blue Men*. It originated during his youth in the form of a recurring dream. Over and over, the mythical creatures that lived in the sea visited his sleep. Throughout the years, Hamish used the visual images to create stories that he shared with all.

Hamish would soon be lowered into the ground; he would dream no more. The community of Barra attended the elder MacNeil's funeral. During the benediction I listened not to the priest, but to my father's "voice" as it echoed in my head. I can "hear" him telling the stories so dear to myself and others. He foretold, "One day, the stories will exist in your heart." It is assumed that, as his son, I will bear the responsibility of keeping the tales alive. An unusual inheritance that requires no written will. My father's "voice" reminded me, "The stories only live in their telling."

Hamish could normally be found in the local pub, a small gathering place that always had a cross-section of the village. The old and young, dogs underneath bar stools, musicians, and, of course, a storyteller. To honor him, I carry on the tradition. My first telling, *The Blue Men*, would be before a small audience at his wake. A silence falls over the room before I begin:

Rough seas are embraced by the foolish, and calm waters belong to the wise. As a young man, I often rowed to the mainland of Scotland from the Isle of Barra. The seas of the Little Minch are treacherous, and this can be a region of mirage. A man's mind can play tricks in isolation. The present view startles me; I ask myself was it a deception or reality? I then rub the eyes and shake my head, yet the scene remains the same. The creatures surface from underwater, bobbing up and down mimicking the waves motion. There are a dozen of them. They have a glossy blue skin, grey face with curly green hair and a beard. Their eyes are small, noses flat and mouths covered with large whiskers; arms are elongated and legs like fish-tails. They are similar to seals but contain human attributes. I question my own creativity, and conclude that I am incapable of making them up. I stop rowing as the space between us grows smaller. I stare at each one, and they back at me.

In that moment, my mind took me back to Barra. I recalled other captains who told stories of their encounters. At the time, my doubt displayed on my face, I did not believe the seamen. With determination, they proceeded all the same. Over the years, several of them told me that only a clever riddle granted them safe passage. I once inquired about the ones who failed to produce a riddle, and was told the Blue Ones conjured up storms. The travelers were overtaken by the sea.

I had completed this journey many times, and must admit the riddles were always in my thoughts. I turned my boat as one of them spoke, but I did not hear sound. Rather, I can only say that his statement was heard, "We have seen you many times near the dwelling called Kisimul Castle."

I respond, "I am the caretaker of a small region of Barra traveling to Skye for provisions. I live a simple life in a small roundhouse. My name is Hamish, and I spend my days looking after the inhabitants of Castlebay." After an unnerving silence, I ask, "What about your kind?"

They answer in unison as a choir, "We are the Blue Men of the Minch who originate from the sky, but live in the sea. Our bodies are transparent, and we can disappear at will. Those whom we allow to view us say that we are blue, but that is simply light reflecting from the sky. We cannot return from whence we came, and are unable to remain where we are. Constantly restless, we reside in-between sea and sky, land and water, form and void - life and death."

Now that the introductions are out of the way, I am told, "Time to honor tradition, your passage requires a riddle. If you have no riddle, then the sea will swallow your soul. If we solve your riddle, then, as before, you will descend to the depths."

The Blue Ones, together, hold out their webbed hands and state, "We await your words!"

I wipe my brow and take a deep breath:

"I have conquered the sea, saved the world
Won battles, and served as King,
Yet, I have never left the place of my creation."

"What Am I?"

I raised my eyebrows and waited. Thankfully, the only sound that returned to me was the lapping of the waves.

Then, they ask, "What is the solution?"

"The imagination!"

We all had a laugh, and with that I was granted passage. They spoke one last time stating that we would meet again, not in the waters but in the place of images and dreams. With that, The Blue Ones vanished in an instant.

I survived the encounter unscathed - or so I believed.

However, the Blue Men continued to come uninvited into my dreams each night, consuming my sleep.

The first of them coming on the harvest moon, each successive dream found the clansmen of Barra facing less to eat.

The Blue Men then dragged seaweed to the shore, and spread it on the fields for fertilizer. In return, the villagers were to light a candle and pour ale into the sea. Because of the odd requests, it took me a while to convince my countrymen. Eventually, we parted with some of our precious alcohol, pouring it as instructed. Thereafter, seaweed appeared and crops improved. We repeated the ritual once every year at hallowtide which signals the close of harvest and the beginning of winter.

Stories of other riddles required for passage continue to surface, albeit not as frequently as in the past.

To end the story, I gather the children before me. I instruct them to hold out their hands. Looking at each one, I say, "Centuries ago several wee-ones belonging to the Hebrides Islands were born with webbed hands, a testament that relations between the Blue Men and our ancestors were once much closer." A thorough examination reveals no webs, but I wonder how many of them have blue blood flowing in their Highland veins.

Later that evening, I returned to my father's house, a round structure made of stone with windows that give view to the surrounding fields. Before falling asleep, I reflect back, believing the audience received my words well. I smile with hope that my father was pleased. It is late morning before I awake; I put on some tea and remember a new dream from the night before.

My father and I are in the land of my ancestors, on his face a smile of revelation. His voice narrates; he tells me that I am now a storyteller with a duty to give life to words and meaning to tradition, and by so doing, the storyteller fills the voids of human existence. The role is a gift, passed down through the generations granted to those of imagination. With those words the dream ends; although, on occasion I expect to "hear" from him.

Fully, awake I sip tea while listening to the gears of the clock grind the future into past. That afternoon, I leave the Island of Barra on the ferry traveling to Oban. My residence is in Glasgow, and I would not live the life of my father. My feet crave the cobblestone streets of the city, not the earth of Barra. However, I visit Castlebay frequently to retell the stories, born out of dreams, trapped by the heart, put to words, then released to the world.

Clouds over the Hill

The Little Minch

Kisimul Castle

1030 Neil of the Castle builds a stronghold in Castlebay.
1200's Much of the current castle dates to.
1263 The MacNeils lead the men of Barra to victory over the Norse at the Battle of Largs.
1314 Fighting in the Wars for Scottish Independence, Clan MacNeil led the men of Barra to a Scottish victory against England at the Battle of Bannockburn.
1651 The clan fights at The Battle of Worcester where English and Scottish Royalists loyal to King Charles II are defeated by the English Parliamentary forces of Oliver Cromwell.
1689 The clan fights at The Battle of Killiecrankie where Jacobite Royalists (Highlanders and Irish) achieve victory over Orange Covenanters (Highlanders and Lowlanders).
1715 The clan supports the Jacobite Rising.
1840 The 40th chief, Roderick, goes bankrupt and is forced to sell Barra and all his lands to the Gordons of Cluny. The castle soon passed to the Cathcarts by marriage.
1937 The castle is purchased by the MacNeils of Barra. The structure undergoes restoration by the American architect Robert Lister MacNeil (1889-1970).
2000 Kisimul Castle was leased to Historic Scotland for a thousand years. The annual rent is £1 and a bottle of whiskey.

Castlebay 8" x 10" oil

ROTHESAY CASTLE
8" x 10" oil

Family / Clan Associations:
Stewart

Rothesay Castle overlooks the Firth of Clyde from the Isle of Bute. Perched on Barelegs Mound, the circular fortress is protected by a moat fed from nearby Loch Fad. The castle suffered numerous sieges from its origins in 1098. From the eleventh to the fourteenth century, ownership passed back and forth, first between Norway and Scotland, then between England and Scotland; but from 1334 on, the island and castle were under Scottish control. The castle suffered additional sieges in 1462, 1527, 1544, and 1650, and was finally destroyed in 1685; it was partially rebuilt in 1816. The painting is based on a 2008 artist's visit.

Invasions

A Legend of Rothesay Castle

Many of Scotland's castles not only changed ownership between native clans, but were attacked, sometimes constructed and even owned by surrounding nations. Rothesay Castle, located on the Isle of Bute, passed between Norwegian, English, and Scottish control. The castle has remained under the Scottish flag since 1334, but the ruins of this noble structure date back to the 1200's.

Bute was settled by Norseman at the end of the eighth century with longhouses surviving into the twelfth century. Norwegian control of the lands was formalized in 1098, when King Edgar of Scotland signed the island over to King Magnus III of Norway. The Norwegians called Bute and the surrounding islands the 'Sudreys' (Southern Islands).

By 1200, Bute was held by the Scottish Alan, King William I's steward. Alan's family was of Anglo-Norman origin. During this age, Scotland operated under a feudal system whereby lords and barons were granted extensive tracts of land in return for performing service to the king. Rothesay, an important part of the feudalism, served as both a fortified residence, and also a status symbol granted to those the king entrusted.

Before 1230, Rothesay Castle returned to Norwegian control. The castle's outer wall was built of stone, and the entire structure was modeled after a previous structure made of earth and timber. In that same year, Haakon IV of Norway appointed Uspak as King of Man and the Isles. He was soon sent to Bute with a fleet to claim the island including the castle. The siege lasted three days during which time the Norwegians attacked the soft rock walls by hewing them with axes. They protected themselves with shields made of wood, although the Norwegians suffered heavy losses before winning the castle.

However, their lairdship over the isle was short-lived as two-hundred Scottish ships under Alan of Galloway were sighted to the south. The Norwegians withdrew to the nearby Kintyre Peninsula. According to Scottish and Manx accounts, Uspak died from wounds received during the battle for Rothesay. The castle was back in Scottish hands, but the ownership would not last.

King Haakon led another expedition in 1263. His stated purpose: *To avenge the warfare of his dominions*. The Scots defending Rothesay yielded in return for a truce; once outside the castle walls, most were killed. Soon thereafter, the Scottish King, Alexander III refused to renounce his claim to the Islands of Bute, Arran, and the Cumbraes. What followed was the inconclusive Battle of Largs in November of 1263. The battle was fought on the mainland directly across from the Isle of Bute. Alexander Stewart directed the Scottish forces, and Haakon eventually retreated and died on his return journey. He was buried at Kirkwall on the Orkney Islands which served as the Norwegian base of operations.

Three years later, in 1266, by the Treaty of Perth, King Magnus (Haakon's son) handed over the Kingdom of Man and the Western Isles. The Treaty outlined a substantial payment to Magnus, and ended the military conflict between Norway, under Magnus, *The Law-Mender,* and Scotland, under King Alexander III. The treaty required an initial payment of four-thousand marks (a measure of weight used mainly for gold and silver) and an annuity of one-hundred marks paid during the subsequent decades. Scotland also concededed Norwegian sovereignty over the Shetland and Orkney Islands. The Isle of Bute was now officially part of the Scottish Kingdom and fortifications at Rothesay Castle were updated by the addition of the projecting gatehouse containing a portcullis and four rounded projecting towers.

Rothesay became an important castle during the Wars of Scottish Independence fought between the Kingdoms of Scotland and England. The castle was held by the English, but was re-captured by Robert the Bruce in 1311. It again fell to the English in 1334, but was quickly retaken by the Scots.

The fortress figured prominently in the rise of the Stewarts, a dynasty that produced Scotland's kings from 1371 to 1542. Rothesay Castle became a favorite residence of Kings Robert II and Robert III who died at the castle in 1406. Robert II granted hereditary stewardship of the castle to his son, the ancestor of the Earls and Marquises of Bute. In 1401, Robert III made his eldest son, David, the Duke of Rothesay. The heir of the title, honoring tradition, was awarded the throne of Scotland. Throughout the eleventh to the fourteenth century, the castle played a central role in the politics of Scotland, both in defining a nation's geography and as a residence of kings.

Rothesay Castle

1098 Magnus Barelegs (1073-1103), King of Norway, Hebrides and Man builds the first wooden castle on the Isle of Bute.
1100's The stone castle is constructed consisting of a keep with four massive round towers surrounded by a moat.
1200's Bute becomes part of the Scottish Kingdom when King William the Lion (1142-1214) seized control of the Firth of Clyde.
1230 Uspak, the Viking King of Man and the Isles besieged the Scots at Rothesay.
1263 The castle is captured by King Haakon of Norway before he was defeated at the Battle of Largs. The Stewarts are keepers of the castle.
1266 The Viking threat passes with the Treaty of Perth. The Isle of Man and the Hebrides become Norwegian territories at a time when Scotland and Norway were still forming themselves as nation-states.
1290's The castle falls to King Edward I (1239-1307) of England.
1306 The Scots recover Rothesay with a force from the sea led by Sir Robert Boyd of Cunningham.
1332 At the Battle of Dupplin Moor where the Bruce is defeated by Balliol, Rothesay is again English held for King Edward III (1312-1377). Backed by the English King, Edward Balliol (d. 1367), is intermittently King of Scotland from 1332 to 1336. In 1334, the castle is re-taken by the Scots.
1401 King Robert III (1340-1406) makes his son David, the Duke of Rothesay.
1406 King Robert III (c.1340-1406) dies at Rothesay.
Late 1400's A large rectangular keep and gatehouse are added.
1462 The castle is besieged by the Earl of Ross.
1527 The Master of Ruthven sieges the castle.
1541 The castle, built for both for comfort and defense, is completed by King James V (1512-1542).
1544 Rothesay Castle is captured by the Earl of Lennox on behalf of the English.
1650's The castle is held for King Charles I (1600-1649), but later falls to Cromwell (1559-1658). His men damage the castle.
1685 The Earl of Argyll's forces torch the castle.
1816 The castle is repaired and partially rebuilt.
1951 The Crichton-Stuart Marquises of Bute move to Mount Stuart located further south on the island. Rothesay Castle is placed in the care of the state and managed by Historic Scotland.

Bridge over the Motte

Gatehouse, Rothesay Castle

The Chapel at Rothesay Castle

SCONE PALACE
8" X 10" oil

**Family / Clan Associations:
Ruthven and Murray**

The history of Scone Palace began when Celtic holy men, the Culdees, established a community of monks there during the seventh century. Over four-hundred years later, in 1114, Alexander I founded an Augustian Abbey on the site. The Stone of Destiny, used in the coronation of Scotland's kings, was brought to Scone by Scotland's first king, Kenneth MacAlpine (843 to 860.) Ten Scottish Parliaments sat at the Palace between 1284 and 1401, their enactment of each new law marked by the ringing of the bell at Scone Abbey. In 1384, after slaying his Comyn rival in Dumfries, Robert the Bruce traveled to Scone in an attempt to legitimize his bid for power. A new structure was built in 1580 after the Protestant Reformation, and most of the current Palace dates from 1802. The painting depicts its appearance in 2004.

The Destiny of a Nation

A Legend of Scone Palace

A man on horseback passes swiftly in front of the chapel at Scone, his cloak bearing obvious marks of royalty. The horse's hooves pierce the earth, flinging clumps of dirt into the air. He rides to a ceremony, the crowning of the King. Like all the nobles of Scotland, he will bring a small portion of dirt from his own region of the realm. When all have added their handfuls to Moot Hill, where the coronation takes place, the new King will be crowned, standing astride (as it were) the whole nation. In another age, the King might have traveled all around Scotland. In this case, all Scotland came to the King. At least that was the scene five-hundred years ago, when the Abbey at Scone was considered the heart of the Scottish nation.

The coronation ceremony required a king to stand on the Stone of Scone, otherwise known as the Stone of Destiny. Off-white in color, square, and neither polished nor elegantly carved, the stone bore two large iron rings, one each on opposite sides. Kings were crowned while standing atop the stone that represents the nation of Scotland. Furthermore, wherever the stone resides, the nation of Scotland is present. If the stone is in another country, then according to tradition Scotland rules it. But given the diversity of such stories, and the obscurity of their origin, what better place to seek the truth about the stone than a Scottish pub? And in nearby Perth, I quickly found a perfect one.

Surveying the crowd, I located two men stationed at the bar. Youth clearly fled them decades ago; I was confident that they would have stories to spin. I pulled up a stool, and one of their other cronies joined us. My accent gave my tourist status away, no doubt, as I asked them about the Stone of Scone. I discovered several versions through the compelling arguments of the three Scotsmen.

They presented no credentials, but I was assured they were all experts (self-proclaimed) regarding the topic. One was named Alastair, the other William; Peter was the late arrival. Though they all spoke at once, it was Peter's voice that I heard, "The stone is Jacob's pillow from when he saw the angels of Bethel. Our rock is sacred and was brought here from the Holy Land."

In Scottish brogue, shaking his finger, Alastair retorted, "No, no, it is from a Roman altar taken out of Antonine's Wall."

William added his version, "The stone came from Ireland, and was held at Dunstaffnage Castle on the western coast before coming to Scone. The first king to unite Scotland, MacAlpine, brought it from Ireland."

Peter responded, "The stone was never at Dunstaffnage and has always been at Scone. It crowned Scottish Kings, and the monks gave Edward a fake! The real one remains hidden."

The conversation was moving quickly. (To afford some background: King Edward of England removed the stone from Scotland to England's Westminster Abby in 1307. He had a coronation chair specially built so that English Kings' feet would rest upon it.)

William continued, "The real stone was given to Edward and taken to England."

Alastair questioned that, "Then why did he return two years later ransacking Scone? What was he looking for then?"

"That clever monk gave him the privy cover!" responded Alastair.

He continued, "In 1996, when the stone was returned to Scotland, we got our privy cover back. It had been missing for three-hundred years. England had the real one; the Scottish Nationalists had stolen it in 1950, made a copy and left it in Arbroath. The stone currently displayed in Edinburgh Castle is a copy made in 1950." He smiles, "Only the Nationalists know where the authentic stone is hidden."

I was almost dizzy trying to keep up. A couple of more pints kept them talking, and the banter continued late into the night. Each version was vigorously defended, and in the end, I learned no more then I had already discovered: there are as many stories as there are Scots.

In a pub environment, it is difficult to even find one that agrees with himself! The facts in these historical issues have given themselves over to legends long ago, and any version of the story can be passed off as genuine – especially, in a Scottish pub!

The next morning, I returned to Scone to study the rock. What a great story it would be if this copy turned out to be the real one. I laughed inside, thinking how very Scottish that would be: the genuine article, hiding all the while directly in front of us all! With no guards, and no security, a person could just take it - if they could lift it, that is. Still, no one bothered with this forgery; here it stood, in view of passing tourists.

I watched a couple of young lads, out of reach of authority, run to the stone. The younger of them stood proudly, announcing to all, "I am the King of Scotland." His older brother laughed and quickly pushed him off stepping upon the stone to proclaim himself King. I had to think: since another name for the symbol is the Stone of Destiny, perhaps this child will someday rule the nation.

I did not revisit the pub; but I did learn that regarding the stone it is best to choose a story and stick with it, whatever the version. Perhaps, after all these years, at the Palace or the pub, the facts make no difference; it's only one's own convictions that matter, of course, it helps to be a good story-teller. I took one last look at the stone. I must say, it did look like a privy cover to me.

Scone Palace

By 600 The location is the capital of a small Pictish Kingdom. Before the 700's Celtic holy men, the Culdess, establish a community of monks at Scone.

700-800's The Scots, now in Western Scotland, begin to look east for new lands that are safer from invading Norsemen.

843 The first king of Scots, Kenneth MacAlpin (810-858), absorbs the Pictish kingdom of Scone. The Kingdom of Scotland is traditionally dated to this year.

1100's An abbey is founded at Scone.

Between 1284 – 1401 Scottish Parliaments are held at Scone.

1306 Robert the Bruce (1274-1329) rushed to Scone and crowned King in an effort to legitimize his bid for power after slaying his Comyn rival in Dumfires High Kirk.

1559 The abbey is sacked by a Protestant mob after a sermon by John Knox (1510-1572) in nearby Perth.

1580 The property passed to the Ruthvens.

1580's The Ruthven family constructs a Palace believed to have been built from the previous Abbot's lodging.

1600 Scone passes to the Murrays after the Gowrie Conspiracy. Sir David Murray (d. 1631) had been one of those to save the King's James VI (1566-1625) and others from the Ruthvens.

1602 The Murrays are made Viscounts Stormont.

1715 and 1745, The Murrays of Scone, 5th and 6th Viscounts, were imprisoned for their hospitality to both the *Old Pretender,* James Francis Edward Stuart, and the *Young Pretender*, Prince Charles Edward Stuart, during their bids to claim the throne of Scotland.

1716 James VIII (1688-1766) or James Francis Edward Stuart – The *Old Pretender* holds court at Scone during the Jacobite Risings.

1745 Bonnie Prince Charlie (1720-1788) visits.

1651 The last king inaugurated at Scone is Charles I (1600-1649). He represents the only Presbyterian coronation in British history.

1776 The Murray's are made Earls of Mansfield.

1802 The large castellated mansion, designed by architect William Atkinson (1774-1839), is built.

2000's The Murray of Mansfield and Viscounts Stormont own Scone Palace.

The forest near Scone Palace

Scone Palace

HUNTLY CASTLE
8" X 10" oil

**Family / Clan Associations:
MacDuff, Seton, and Gordon**

Huntly Castle commands the confluence of the Deveron and Strathbogie rivers. Most of what remains today was constructed in 1410, although the castle site dates to 1180. Huntly, sacked in 1452, underwent extensive remodeling in the sixteenth century, transforming it into a baronial mansion. That structure was besieged in 1562 and 1644, and destroyed in 1745. The painting represents a 2004 view of the ruin.

Shadows in the Wind

A Legend of Huntly Castle

Even the rivers refuse to flow swiftly here. The tranquility envelopes all in this place where where past meets present. Town and castle both named Huntly stand upon an ancient burgh. The castle represents time gone by. The small city is rushed and busy, yet cobblestone streets and stone buildings give evidence of another era. The town is modernized with industry, but the castle stands as an ever-present icon of the ages.

An arched gate marks the threshold between old and new. The two realms are as different as night and day. Dwarfed by trees, the ruins of Huntly Castle stand strategically placed between the rivers Deveron and Strathbogie. As shadows dance in a late afternoon breeze, water flows over the rocks. It gives the area around the castle a sense of solace. Faint sounds emanate from the nearby town, cars traveling over the stone streets, children playing soccer in the parks. Noise from the distance disturbs the peace of this place.

The castle, at its height, claimed title as one of the greatest Scottish baronial mansions. Masons were abundant here, and they gave impressive and complex decorations to the stone. An elaborate frieze covers the entire front of the structure, announcing: *George Gordon, Marquis of Huntly*. Directly below presumably is the name of his wife: *Henreitte Stewart, Marquis of Huntly*. Perhaps an old Roman maxim would have been more appropriate: *Your Alliances Determine Your Future*. Hangings, beheadings, and sieges made for a turbulent six-hundred year history.

As allegiances shifted: entire garrisons were lined against the walls and shot, soldiers were hanged from the surrounding trees, and heads tumbled down the gentle hills that cover the landscape. George Gordon lost his own head after finding himself on the wrong side of a battle; being royalty, he was transported to Edinburgh for the axe.

The life that exists in the nearby town once existed here. The residents no doubt busied themselves with the days duties; there were marriages, births and deaths. But the place is now given over to the ghosts, most notably an aberration of a girl who found herself with child, but no husband, and who later committed suicide. All Scotland, it sometimes seems, is populated by ghosts.

There's a great hollowness to this place abandoned so long ago. The ground itself seems empty. Seasons ebb and flow without comment or complaint. What remains is the sound of the river, and the wind through the trees. The shadows move in rhythm as the branches creak, back and forth, against the ancient walls.

Huntly Castle
(Previously known as Strathbogie Castle)

1180 The first castle, the Peel of Strathbogie, is built by Duncan, Earl of Fife. It is constructed atop mound near the present castle.
1307 King Robert the Bruce (1274-1329) is carried to Huntly when he fell ill at the Battle of Inverurie - The Scottish Royal Army battled victoriously against the opponents of Bruce.
1307 King Robert the Bruce stays here before defeating the Comyn Earl of Buchan.
1400's The castle consists of a large round keep. The structure is rectangular in plan with a large round tower at one end.
1410 The castle passes to the Setons then the Gordons in the early 14th century. The Gordon laird replaced the wooden fortress with a stone keep.
1452 The old castle is burned by the Douglas, Earl of Moray during the civil war between the Houses of Stewart and Douglas.
1500's The upper story of the keep was remodeled with decorative stonework, inscribed friezes, and new windows.
1506 In one of the first examples of re-branding, the name was changed from Strathbogie to Huntly. The new name is taken from a Gordon property near the village of Gordon located along the borders region.
1550's The fourth Earl transforms the castle into a Renaissance Palace.
1594 The 6th Earl of Argyll leads a rising against King James VI (1566-1625) and defeats forces under the Earl of Argyll at the Battle of Glenlivet.
1602 Huntly castle is attacked by King James VI and damaged. The castle is quickly repaired.
1640 The castle is occupied by a Covenanting Army that destroys most of the interior.
1644 The castle was taken by the Marquis of Montrose (1612-1650), then captured by General David Leslie (1600-1682) three years later after starving out then slaughtering the garrison.
1647 David Leslie, a Covenanter, captures Huntly hanging and beheading its Irish garrison.
1684 The Marquis is made Duke of Gordon.
1745-46 The castle is garrisoned by the Hanoverian soldiers during the Jacobite Rising.
2000's The castle is managed by Historic Scotland.

Water over the Rocks, near Huntly

CASTLE TIORAM
8" X 10" oil

Family / Clan Associations:
MacDonald of Clanranald

Since the thirteenth century, Castle Tioram has controlled the seaways between the Hebrides and the Isle of Skye. Tioram's curtain wall dates to the fourteenth century. Expanded and fortified in the sixteenth century, the castle withstood sieges in 1554 and 1651, but was destroyed in 1715. The painting illustrates the castle's appearance in 1998.

Central Locations

A Legend of Castle Tioram

The nation of Scotland is surrounded by oceans and seas; lochs trap water on land, and sometimes during rain or fog the moisture appears suspended in the air. Until recently, the rivers, lochs, and oceans served as the passageways of Scotland. The islanders transported themselves and goods on these many waterways. Most castles of Scotland, including Tioram, could be accessed by boat.

A fortress of curtain walls, dating to 1353, is perched on the highest point of Eilean Tioram (the dry island). However, earlier structures did stand on the site. The position was highly defensible almost unassailable. In its long history, the castle was only taken once. Overlooking the Loch of Moidart, Tioram occupied a commanding position controlling the waterways around Loch Shiel to Loch Sunart that captains used to avoid the dangerous waters off Ardnamurchan Point. The structure was protected by water and could only be entered during low tide along a narrow causeway.

During the clan-on-clan warfare of the 1300's, Clan Campbell laid siege to the castle for five weeks. Unsuccessful, the warriors eventually gave up and set sail. The members of Clanranald exited the castle traveling to the mainland for a celebration. Under the cover of night, the Campbells altered their course to the north side. Pulling off a rouse, they quickly overpowered the few men left at guard. The Clanranalds soon returned, overtook the Campbells, and slaughtered them.

During the Jacobite uprising of 1715, the castle was set alight on orders of its owner Allan, the chief of Clanranald. Allan destroyed his own castle as a preventative measure to keep the stronghold from falling into Hanoverian hands. The chief had joined the Standard of the Earl of Mar in support of *The Old Pretender*, James Francis Edward Stuart. Shortly thereafter, he was killed at the Battle of Sheriffmuir (1715) fighting for the Jacobite cause. After the defeat, the clan returned to their lands disheartened by the loss of their chief and castle.

Nevertheless, now into the 2000's, the clan continues on. The chief of the Macdonalds of Clanranald is traditionally designated as *The Captain of Clanranald*. Currently, both the chief and clan are recognized by the Lord Lyon King of Arms – the heraldic judge in Scotland.

Castle Tioram
(Pronounced Cheerum)

1300's A curtain wall rises.
1500's A tower house and ranges of buildings are added.
1386 The Macdonalds of Clan Ranald, Reginald MacDonald, 1st chief, dies at the castle.
1411 Alan, 2nd Chief fought at the Battle of Harlaw where Lowland Clans fought the Allies of the Isles - Highland Clans. The battle was indecisive.
1505 Allan MacDonald, 4th chief, was executed by James IV (1473-1513) after taking part in the pillaging of Atholl - a region in central Scotland.
1544 Ian Moidartch, 8th chief, is kidnapped and held at Edinburgh Castle. He escapes and recovers his lands after Castle Tioram was seized.
1544 Mary de Guise (1515-1560), Regent of Scotland, orders the Earls of Huntly and Argyll to attack the castle.
1651 In an unsuccessful attempt to subdue the wild Papists of the Western Highlands, Cromwell's forces occupy the castle after a siege.
1715 The castle is torched by orders of its last occupant so that Hanoverian forces could not use it. Alan Mor of Clanranarld, 14th Chief of Clan Ranald, leads the left wing of the Jacobite forces and was killed at the Battle of Sheriffmuir – the castle is never reoccupied.
1732 Lady Grange is imprisoned here before allegedly being taken to the outer isles.
1997 The castle is sold to a private party with plans for restoration.

High Tide

DUART CASTLE
8" x 10" oil

**Family / Clan Associations:
Maclean and the Campbells of Argyll**

Duart Castle, a landmark on the Isle of Mull, is perched upon Black Point. The structure sits strategically at the junction of three seaways – the Firth of Lorne, Loch Linnhe, and the Sound of Mull – which enhanced Duart's control of the sea trade between the Hebrides and Ulster, Ireland. The curtain wall that surrounds Duart dates to the thirteenth century. A keep was constructed in 1390; more than a century's worth of additions followed. After a siege by surrounding clans in 1538, the castle underwent expansion into the seventeenth century, only to suffer another more devastating siege in 1745, and abandonment by 1751. The castle was restored in the early 1900's. The painting depicts its appearance in 2006.

Time Stops Here

A Legend of Duart Castle
(Told from the perspective of Ewan Maclean)

I hold a pocket watch out to my side. It swings back and forth dangling on a gold chain. I can see the dial, but the methodical tick, tick, tick cannot be heard over the galloping of the hoofs, the rattle of the bridle, and the neighing of my horse. These sounds along with my name, Ewan Maclean, are what my fellow clansmen fear.

My story begins on the Isle of Mull, the year is 1558. I remember my wife chattering about my small head; in turn, I carry on about her black bottom, so stained because she often sits where we store the peat. My father also comments about my head, but his jests are in regard to my intelligence. I need things repeated, so most regard me as simple. Although the son of the Maclean chief, my skills are not in administration. I spend my days fishing, away from them both. There is no better life than being on the sea looking forward to the next catch.

My father, the leader of the Lochbuie Macleans, is elderly. Time is closing in on him, and it is rumored that his last breaths draw near. I have not visited him recently. My wife, a MacDougall, wants to ensure my inheritance but my claim is challenged. My father has a brother Lachlan who controls the stronger Macleans of Duart. My father grows tired of the constant bickering regarding the estate. To settle the issue, he calls in Lachlan. A heated discussion full of threats ensues. We are unable to resolve any of the issues and in an ironic twist Lachlan challenges me to a duel.

It is the eve of battle and the air is calm and filled with the smells of spring. This peace will soon be replaced by the noise and stench of war. Until then, I savor each breath, knowing by the morning they would be rushed. The light that illuminates the land of my ancestors will soon turn to darkness.

Looking down on the Duart citadel from a small hill, I see smoke rise from a group of blackhouses. I view my friends returning from a hunt while others prepare for fishing. A daily routine unfolds before me in this seaside village. What hangs heavily over the scene is not only the impending duel between Lachlan and me, but a war between competing families the Duart Macleans and the Lochbuie Macleans. The conflict will alter our lives forever.

Turning away from Duart, I take a walk through the nearby woods. There is the sound of a stream as it moves to the sea. A short way into the forest, I see a figure washing clothes. As I get closer, a heaviness fills my heart; but curiosity has taken hold and it is too late to escape; a spell is already cast. This is no mortal, but a demon ringing blood out of a shirt. The creature is clad in a white shawl that drapes over a small head. With each turn of the cloth, the stream flows a deeper red. Through a veil, lies a bony face and skin as shallow as the water that runs beneath. Turning toward me, the creature's piercing eyes take me captive; I stand motionless.

Death is before me, although I feel my heart pumping with the blood of life. Realms collide: and how could I, a simple mortal, understand the immortal? This minion of the devil exists in the beyond, but I live in the here and now. Fear fills my heart, as the creature grinds its teeth while clicking its fingernails in rhythm.

The demon looks not at me but directly through me to the village beyond. There is an emptiness in my voice when I ask, "Is this day my last?

It breathes heavily and replies, "The sun is setting on the world as it has everyday before; tomorrow, the sun will set on your world as it never has before."

There is a long silence before I speak. "Then, you have come for me?"

It continues twisting the shirt and slowly answers, "Eventually, I come for all."

Our conversation ends as I slowly walk backwards down the trail. I never take my eyes off the creature as it continues the work. Emerging from the forest, I move along the shore, before stopping where the water meets the sand, watching the sun descend into the sea.

My thoughts allow me no rest, I am up all night. Sitting near the fire in our blackhouse, with forehead pressed against my sword. I review in my head, again and again, my encounter with the demon. It is not long until the morning light overcomes the night. I see that all the clan members have gathered for battle.

The sun continues its rise over the horizon as this day of tragedy begins. Time stops as I lose a sense of place in the disorder of war. Caught up in all the action, I fail to realize that I am standing in the creek, at the exact spot I had met the demon the day before. In a moment of distraction, undefended, I am uprepared for the enemy's sword that buries itself in my skull. I feel the warmth of my own blood cover my eyes as it flows down my shirt into the water. Through a scarlet mist, I see walking toward me, slowly, step by deliberate step, the angel of death. My senses begin to leave me. Somehow, I manage to rise, stumble, and mount my horse. Beginning to trot, I look back to where the demon stood. He is searching for the corpse he had been summoned to collect. My breaths slow to a stop; I slump, and die in the saddle. My head, detached, falls to the ground, rolling like a boulder down a hill.

Though dead, I continue to "live." Because I have not perished where destiny prescribed, I am cursed to become an omen: The Horseman of Mull, riding around the isle for eternity, residing in the world of the in-between, waiting on the death of those alive. I am a slave to the demon. The clatter of a hoof, the galloping of a horse, are sounds feared by the living. I travel around and harvest the souls of the Macleans. Those that have lived in charity, justice, and truth, I have no claim on; however, those that have lived in greed, envy, and pride are mine to deliver. My first is that of *Black Bottom*. For all those years, I belonged to her; and now she belongs to me.

In one hand, my small head dangles back and forth, held by the hair. In the other, time itself hangs on a gold chain swinging methodically with each tick. I ride across Glen Mor forever, as immortal as the seasons.

Duart Castle

1200's Duart consists of a large curtain wall encloses a courtyard on a rocky knoll.
1300's The castle is under the control of the Clan Maclean.
1390 Lachlan Lubanach, 5th chief (c. 1350, died before 1405), built a keep adjoining the outside wall enclosing the existing well.
1390 The first known charter for Duart is dated 1390. The granddaughter of Robert II (1316-1390), King of Scots lists Duart as her dowry.
1411 The 6th chief, *Red Hector*, was killed while fighting with the MacDonalds at the Battle of Harlaw where Lowland Clans fought the allies of the Isles (Highland Clans). The battle was indecisive.
1500's A range of three stories is added.
1520's Lachlan Cattanach (c. 1465-1527) chains his barren wife, Margaret Campbell to a rock in the hopes that she would drown. She is rescued by passing fisherman. Her Campbell relatives take their revenge, killing Lachlan in 1527.
1538 Ewen Maclaine of Lochbuie is beheaded in battle, his ghost, the headless horseman haunts the Island of Mull.
1600's Another three-storey block is added.
1608 Chief Lachlan was kidnapped after dinner with the King's Lord Lieutenant on board a Royal ship. Lachlan gains his freedom after a destruction of his war galleys and an oath of fealty to King James VI (1566-1625).
1653 A passing storm sinks two of Cromwell's besieging ships.
1645 Duart Castle briefly serves as a garrison for Hanoverian troops.
1647 The castle is sacked by General Leslie (1600-1682).
1650's The Macleans of Duart lose more men aiding the Royalist cause principally in the 1651 Battle of Inverkeithing where the Scottish Army supporting King Charles II suffered defeat by the English Parliamentarian Army.
1674 The Campbells of Argyll acquire the castle.
1689 The Macleans remained staunch supporters of the Stewarts through the Jacobite Risings and fought at the Battle of Killiecrankie where Highlander and Irish Jacobites achieved victory over the Orange Covenanter Royalists (Highlander and Lowlanders).
1745 The castle is torched by Hanoverian troops and is abandoned. It soon becomes
roofless and derelict.
1911- 1936 Duart is acquired and restored by Fitzroy MacLean (1835-1936).
2000's The castle is owned by the Macleans of Duart and Morvern.

Black Point, The Isle of Mull

DUNSTAFFNAGE CASTLE
9" x 12" oil

**Family / Clan Associations:
MacDougall and Campbell**

Today, the castle's location adjoins the mainland; but Dunstaffnage Castle originally sat on an small island in Loch Etive. The castle, a Kings of Dalraidia stronghold, was the resting place for The Stone of Destiny (the rock upon which Scotland's kings were crowned). The castle seen today began in 1225; it suffered siege in 1309. The keep, completed in the sixteenth century, is nestled behind a sixty foot curtain wall. In 1685, the castle was destroyed. The painting captures a 2008 vantage.

Alliances

A Legend of Dunstaffnage Castle

Battles and murders changed the alliances that defined the early 1300's in Scotland. On March 27th 1306, Robert the Bruce was crowned King of Scotland at Scone Palace. By June, Bruce suffered defeat at the Battle of Methven by the Earl of Pembroke, an English Governor of Perth. Only five-hundred Scottish soldiers survived out of a force of 4,500 led by Robert. The English lost approximately six-hundred out of three-thousand men. Bruce and the survivors of his army retreated to the Perthshire hills. Here, they were attacked by fellow Scots from Clan MacDougall and Clan MacNab, led by clan chief, John MacDougall of Lorne.

In addition to the defeat at Methven, Bruce's claim to the throne was challenged after he murdered his rival, John Comyn (The Red Comyn) at Greyfriars Kirk in Dumfries. Comyn had an extensive network of family and friends who, with his murder, were then obligated to fight with the English against Bruce. John MacDougall, the maternal uncle of the Red Comyn was himself a claimant to the Scottish throne. Looking to kill the Bruce, John was honoring the blood feud that began with the murder.

During one attack, a MacDougall fought directly with the King. Amidst the struggle, a clansmen grabed the Bruce's plaid and despite being wounded forced him towards the attackers. The King freed himself by releasing the plaid and broach, items that became a trophy for the MacDougalls. Robert's attacker died; Bruce survived the combat, taking refuge with his men in Glen Falloch before moving on.

After their initial confrontations, the MacDougalls and Bruces continued to skirmish. The MacDougall Chief and John's father, Alexander of Lorne, remained a firm supporter of King Edward II of England, who opposed the Bruce. Clan MacDougall twice sent their allies after Bruce, first at Rannoch and then Glenerochty. Both missions failed to kill him and ended in their own defeat. Bruce and his supporters were again struck, this time at Loch Rannoch with a larger force. Robert then went on the offensive, with plans to attack the MacDougalls. Their stronghold was at Dunstaffnage Castle, a highly defensible structure protected by a massive curtain wall over sixty feet high in some places. The fortress, located on an island in the Firth of Lorne, was clearly capable of withstanding siege; however, Bruce would be attacked in the summer of 1308, before reaching the castle.

Unbeknownst to Bruce, the MacDougall army had planned an ambush. Leaving the safety of Dunstaffnage, their familiarity with the terrain allowing the clansmen to reposition themselves in a concealing fog, the MacDougalls laid in wait for Bruce at the Pass of Brander. A short distance from the castle, the pass lies on the thoroughfare between Oban and Tyndrum, where the River Awe rushes past the base of Ben Cruichan. John MacDougall was to defend the high ground on the mountain's north slopes and push boulders on Bruce's advancing forces.

Bruce's army entered the Pass of Brander under a cloud of arrows to fight a desperate battle where the waters of Loch Awe escape to the sea. But the Bruce's superior guerilla tactics, in a narrow field, overpowered the MacDougalls and forced them to break formation. Many drowned while others were slaughtered at the Bridge of Awe. After victory, Bruce continued his march to the western coast where he quickly gained Dunstaffnage. Atypically, he did not destroy it but rather named it a crown castle. The stewardship was granted to Clan Campbell who were loyal to his cause.

In the years following the Battle, Alexander MacDougall is on record as attending a Scottish Parliament, held at St. Andrews, in 1309. One year later, both he and his son, John, had entered the service of King Edward II of England. Alexander is believed to have died in late 1310. John remained in English service attending a royal council at Westminster. He was put in charge of English fleets in 1311 and 1314. In 1315, he conquered the Isle of Man for the English Crown and began receiving a pension from Edward II of England in 1316, the same year of his death.

Robert the Bruce remained King of the Scots until his death in 1329. He is remembered as one of Scotland's greatest kings and a famous warrior for leading the nation during the Wars of Scottish Independence against the Kingdom of England.

Dunstaffnage Castle remained under Campbell control. In 1470, castle ownership officially transferred to the first Earl of Argyll, Colin Campbell. The hereditary Campbell captain remains keeper of the fortress these many centuries later. The castle and nearby chapel no longer sit on an island, but are connected to the mainland. The gatehouse remains closed, reserved for occasional use by the current captain.

Dunstaffange Castle

600's The current castle is built on a fortified site once held by the Kings of Dalriada.
1225 A castle consisting of a massive curtain wall with round towers is built by the MacDougalls, Lords of Lorn.
1308 The castle is captured by King Robert the Bruce (1274-1329) after the MacDougalls are defeated at the Battle of The Pass of Brander.
1309 King Robert the Bruce made the castle a crown property with Clan Campbell as keepers.
1322 The captainship of Dunstaffnage is first entrusted to a Campbell with periods of resurgent MacDougall and Stewart influence in the area, the hereditary post has remained with the Campbells.
1455 The 9th Earl of Douglas fled here to obtain help from the Lord of the Isles after King James II (1430-1460) destroys the power of the Black Douglases.
1470 After six years of clan feuding, the MacDougalls surrender the Lordship of Dunstaffnage and Lorne to the Campbells of Argyll.
1500's A gatehouse is constructed.
1685 The 9th Earl of Argyll burns the castle.
1715 and 1746 Government troops occupy the castle during the Jacobite Risings (1689-1746). Flora MacDonald (1722-1790) is briefly imprisoned here after helping Bonnie Prince Charlie (1720-1788).
1725 A two story house is added and altered during the 1800's.
1958 The castle is put in the care of the state and managed by Historic Scotland.

Curtain Walls, 60 ft. high

Dunstaffnage Chapel

Pass of Brandor

SCOTLAND: CASTLES & CLANS THE LEGENDS

URQUHART CASTLE
8" x 10" oil

Family / Clan Associations:
Urquhart, Durward, Comyn, Gordon, Grant, and MacDonald

A Celtic fortress has occupied Strone Point from the 500's. What is now the ruin of Urquhart Castle began in the 1250's but was besieged, rebuilt, and altered through time. The thirteenth and fourteenth centuries saw substantial expansion, and in the sixteenth century the owners constructed a large keep named the Grant Tower. The castle was destroyed in 1692. The painting depicts a 1998 view.

The Sign of the Cross

A Legend of Urquhart Castle

From the Abbey that he founded on the Isle of Iona, the holy man, St. Columba, journeys to the north of Scotland. Loch Ness is his destination, where he is to meet with the King of the Picts. The year is 580. Upon arrival, Columba is greeted by the Pictish people he will transform. Known as Scotland's oldest inhabitants, the Picts receive their name from the Romans, who called them Picti – *Painted Ones*. Columba arrives at the estate of Airdchartdan, or Urqhart (the present castle location), and meets with a Pictish noble who is descended from a long line of lords. The nobleman's name is Emchath and he is on his death bed. Listening to Columba and believing the word of God, Emchath is baptized and shortly thereafter joins the ranks of the departed. The Saint then baptizes the entire household before moving on to another challenge – a great water beast.

Columba wears a prayer shawl that matches a blue robe circled with a white fringe above his feet. He carries a long staff with a hook on the end, and he often raises it, along with his right hand, to conjure up the powers from beyond. Columba and his party are at the River Ness that flows from the Loch. It is here that another death scene is unfolding. An accident has occurred, leading to a quick burial. The gravediggers say that the man was swimming when he was seized, then bitten, by a water beast that remains in the area. The holy man orders one of his companions, a monk named Lunge, to swim across the river and retrieve a boat. The monk obeys without delay. Not long after he enters the water, the monster surfaces with a gaping mouth, roaring, and rushing towards Lunge with great purpose. The onlookers are struck dumb and are frozen with terror, all but Columba. Raising his staff, he commands the savage-beast, "Do not touch the man and turn back speedily." The beast retreats, as though he were pulled back with ropes of incredible force. The Brothers are amazed and glorify God.

Sightings of the Loch Ness Monster continue into modern times. Only the ruins of Urquhart Castle remain, although it was once a substantial and important Highland stronghold. Columba is remembered as the *Apostle of the Picts* because he evangelized the Islands and Highlands of Scotland. His base was Iona, a small island off the west coast of Scotland located directly above Northern Ireland. Later, Iona became the burial place for kings and queens.

Urquhart Castle
(Pronounced Urkurt)

500's The Picts occupy a fort on Strone Point.
After 1228 The first castle is built by the Durwards. The structure contains a curtain wall, gatehouse, great hall, and a chapel.
After 1275 The Comyns add a large main courtyard.
1296 Castle Urquhart is held by the English forces, by 1297 the castle is liberated by the Scottish Forbes.
1303 King Edward I (1274-1329) of England recaptures Urquhart Castle slaughtering Forbes along with his starving supporters.
1306 King Robert the Bruce (1274-1329) captures the castle killing the English defenders.
1333 The castle is held for Scotland in the name of King David II (1324-1371) against King Edward Balliol (1283-1367) and Edward III of England (1312-1377).
After 1390 Urquhart Castle is held by the Scottish Crown, whose soldiers defend it against attacks by the Scottish MacDonald Lord of the Isles.
1400's Stewart Kings invest in the castle transforming it into a complex fortification with a double towered gatehouse, high keep, and separate citadel.
From 1437 Due to its location on the border of the Western Principality and the Scottish Kingdom, the castle is subject to yearly assaults as a result of clan against clan warfare.
1437 The Earl of Ross captures Urquhart Castle.
1452 The castle is taken by a MacDonald.
1456 The castle becomes a crown property.
1476 The castle is given to the Gordon, Earl of Huntly.
1495 The MacDonald Lordship, who continually attacked the castle, is crushed. Thereafter, Confederations of Western Clans threaten the castle.
In 1509 James IV (1473-1513) gives the castle to John Grant of Freuchie on condition that he strengthens it – the Grants build the tower house.
1513 The castle is attacked after the Scottish defeat by the English at the Battle of Flooden.
1515 The MacDonalds capture the castle, after the death of their enemy, James IV who was killed at the Battle of Flooden.
1544-1545 The MacDonalds with their allies, the Camerons of Lochiel, devastate the castle and surrounding areas.
1644 The castle is sacked by Covenanters.
1689 Urquhart Castle held out against the Jacobites.
1691 The castle is destroyed to prevent Jacobites from using it.
2004 The property is given to the National Trust for Scotland and managed by Historic Scotland.

EILEAN DONAN CASTLE
42.5" x 42.5" oil

**Family / Clan Associations:
Mackenzie and Macrae**

Parts of Eilean Donan Castle date to the thirteenth century, the keep to the fourteenth century. The island fortress was besieged in 1539. In 1719, the Spanish Crown, in support of the Jacobite cause, sent three-hundred troops to garrison Eilean Donan, prompting the English to dispatch their frigates to Loch Duich to destroy the castle. During the twentieth century, the current structure rose from the rubble, rebuilt according to the original plans. Eilean Donan is the most photographed castle in Scotland. The painting is from an artist's visit in 2004.

Lines of Sight

A Legend of Eilean Donan Castle
(Told from the perspective of Ninian Maclennar)

If only for a moment, the morning light reveals a world to me; soon, the fog covers it again. A mist in the air attaches itself to everything on land. The salt from the sea moves into the atmosphere, and during days such as these, there is a taste to the very air. Life here is cold, wet, and at times, dark.

It is early in the morning when we depart for a fishing expedition on Loch Duich. As on most days before, we will pass the Island of Donan. Our progress is cautious due to limited visibility. Moving slowly in the sea, we glimpse the island's great castle by bits, according to the in and out of the haze and the up and down of the waves. It is we who usually look at the castle, but today the castle looks back. The chatter that normally fills our trip is replaced, on this occasion, by an unnerving silence. The heads of the recently executed are displayed atop the castle walls; first hidden and then revealed in the swirling fog, each new set of eyes pierces us to the bone. Though we are guilty of no crimes, we are convicted by their stares; they seem to protest that we are alive when they are dead.

Our boat drifts around the Island. The only sounds are that of the ravens circling their victuals, and several birds are already feasting on the skulls. Looking back, on a sun-lit castle, we see what must be fifty heads methodically placed. With difficulty, we try to return to the business of the day; very few words are exchanged. Perhaps to escape a sense of the presence of the dead, our party ventures beyond familiar precincts. While we would normally catch many fish, we take few this time; none of us is focused. The day is long and the dread of the return trip weighs heavy. We decide to take the long way around, skirting a castle that is so stark with the spectacle of death.

Back in the community and eager for answers, good or bad, we turn to one another. Various explanations are ventured, but the most believable revolve around a new face at Donan - Thomas Randolph, the Earl of Moray and Warden of Scotland. He has arrived on order from the new King – Robert the Bruce. The beheadings are an end to a long twenty five year old story: Robert the Bruce was once, given shelter at the castle after a defeat; and the Bruce's visions of the future are built on alliances from the past. The King has sent Thomas to Eilean Donan; his crown officer loses no time quickly beheading fifty local scoundrels whose skulls now decorate the castle battlements. Perhaps the laird of the castle, a Mackenzie, has given the actual order, or maybe Bruce himself is tidying up his kingdom. In any event, all note that a changing of the guard had been posted. I spend the night

Hidden Entrances

thankful that all of the Maclennar villagers are accounted for!

The next morning many fishermen are back in the boat. Onshore, I only glance once at the castle and not into any of the eyes. Thomas' "justice" has put us all on warning. The only thoughts I have revolve around the unreliability of all political alliance.

Eilean Donan Castle

1200's Upon the shores of Loch Duich, a structure consists of a wall surrounding a courtyard.
1300's A keep of three stories rises.
1263 King Alexander III (1249-1286) gives the lands to Colin Fitzgerald, son of the Irish Earl of Desmond and Kildare, for his help in defeating King Haakon and the Norseman at the Battle of Largs. The family changed their name to Mackenzie – the castle becomes their stronghold.
1306 King Robert the Bruce (1274-1329) is sheltered here.
1331 Randolph, Earl of Moray (d.1332), executes fifty men at the castle.
1504 Eilean Donan Castle is captured by the Earl of Huntly.
1509 The Macraes become constables of the castle.
1539 The castle is besieged by Donald Grumach (or Gorm) MacDonald, a claimant to the Lordship of the Isles. Gorm is killed by an arrow allegedly shot from Duncan Macrae.
1719 William Mackenzie, 5th Earl of Seaforth (d. 1746), had the castle garrisoned with Spanish troops. Three English frigates sail into Loch Duich and quickly destroy the stronghold.
1900's Eilean Donan is completely rebuilt according to historic design.
1983 The castle is managed by the Conchra trust formed by the Macrae family.

Low Tide

Loch Ness

BLAIR CASTLE
8" x 10" oil

Family / Clan Associations:
Comyn, Murray of Atholl and Stewart of Atholl

Blair Castle stands in the center of Scotland, controlling the routes through the Cairngorm Mountains and north to Inverness. The first keep was constructed in 1269; a number of expansions and fortifications were added through the centuries. After the siege of 1654, Blair was remodeled in the eighteenth century. It holds distinction as the last castle to undergo siege (1745) in Britain. In 1842 and 1844, Victoria and Albert stayed at the castle under the protection of a hundred Atholl Highlanders. Victoria was so impressed by the men that she presented them with regimental colors, which allows the Atholl Highlanders private army status. The painting depicts Blair's appearance in 2006.

Seasons

A Legend of Blair Castle

A moon looms large and high in the night sky. The harvest is complete, signaling the end of summer. Days are shorter as winter approaches, and the impending weather change alters our routines. Villagers are occupied with storing provisions; the deer are healthy and traveling in large herds. Nature rewards the prepared, and I grow anxious anticipating the next hunt.

Soon, we will receive word from our chief and begin the trek from the north to Glen Tilt. Clansmen will invade an unwelcoming forest that covers the center of our island. From the valleys and into the mountains, our journey will take us into areas beautiful, dark, and hidden. Many others join us from the south, and royalty will arrive from the great white castle of the glen: Blair, home of the Earls of Atholl.

I am standing under the eave of my blackhouse when I hear the announcement through the medium of bagpipes. Everyone understands that we are to follow the piper through the valley. Before I depart, I hold my hand out and up; the rain puddles in my palm. The drops of water dance as I swallow what nature has left in my grasp.

The piper is close now, playing with purpose and gathering followers. Clansmen emerge from the glens in their one piece plaids. I wear the red and green of MacDonald of Keppoch, the subdued colors providing camouflage against the heather. We travel quickly over the land, animated by a predator's spirit.

The hunt will last for days, and as the seasons move with purpose, so would we. I am Leith MacDonald, a tinchel who gathers and directs wildlife. A group of us enter the forest, gradually moving away from one another. Locating a herd, we surround them, close in, and move the animals so as to direct them to the clansmen and deerhounds waiting below. We perform much of our work by maneuvering ourselves into position silently. Once the drove can be directed, it only takes a small sound to cause a stampede. If we do our job well, then even animals as quick and graceful as these meet their end.

My breath is deliberate and rushed from the chase; my lungs ache with the chill of the air. Unlike those of summer, these days contain mist and fog that cover the valleys. The rocks and tree trunks are covered with moss and are wet to the touch. The whole forest moves on a breeze. During the day we hunt, and under the moon we listen to the sennachies (story-tellers). Each attempts to outdo the other, the tales becoming better as the night grows long. Whisky adds a volatile element to it all. The sounds of bagpipes fill the glens. Women braid their hair and smile at strangers – sometimes even me!

We all pay homage to the host Chief; he and his guests enjoy the great spectacle before them. They relax in the comfort of a rustic bower or lunquard, a structure that is built specifically for the occasion and decorated with heather, fir boughs, and rowan berries. A great theatre is before us, nature the backdrop and we the actors.

We are up early the next morning to learn that she, like a talisman, will ride before us. The hunts, a pretext for social gatherings, have attracted our Queen - Mary. It is August of 1564, and here she is, parading before us; we offer our homage in silence. I will never forget this vision; she is tall, over six feet. At the tender age of twenty-two, she is already a widow; even in her sadness, she is magnificent. Every eye is upon her, watching and waiting not only for a woman's smile, but for that of the Queen. Her presence tames the wildness in us; we watch her calmly surveying the falcons and hawks that fly above. Three-thousand Scotsmen, I amongst them, drive wildlife from the surrounding mountains. Waiting below are the hunters with the standard weapons of war - long bows, swords, and spears. By day's end, 360 deer, along with five wolves are taken. However, the Queen is the day's greatest prize, and distraction.

As the sun descends, a light rain begins to fall. I take small drinks out of my hand, accepting that which heaven offers. A small deer lies draped about my shoulders. I stare into the forest in which I have spent so much time, and for another year, yield it back to the spirits within. Out of the black night, rain turns to sleet; then snow begins to float to the ground covering the rocks, trees, and all traces of our intrusions. Approaching my village, I think of nothing other than the Queen and the stories I will tell. Upstream is Keppoch Castle, a landmark that serves as signpost. My glen comes into view. There is no more pleasant thing for my eyes to behold. I am home.

Blair Castle

1263 The Comyns build a castle on lands owned by David Strathbogie, Earl of Atholl (d. 1326). The incursion led to a Comyn eviction.
1336 King Edward III of England (1312-1377) stays at the castle.
1450 The Earldom of Atholl passes to the Stewarts of Balvenie. It is a reward for their efforts against the Douglases and MacDonalds.
1529 King James V (1512-1542) visits the castle.
1564 Mary Queen of Scots (1542-1587) visits the castle.
1629 The castle and lands are granted to John Murray, Master of Tullibardine by marriage.
1653 The castle is besieged, captured and partially destroyed by Colonel Daniel, one of Cromwell's commanders. It is used by Cromwell forces until 1660.
1703 The Earls of Atholl are made Marquises, then Dukes of Atholl. The new Duke proposed the union of the Scottish and English Parliaments. By 1708, he is under house arrest.
1736 The Earls of Atholl gained the sovereignty of the Isle of Man which they held until 1765 when it was given to the crown.
1745 Bonnie Prince Charlie (1720-1788) stays at the castle.
1746 Hanoverian forces occupy the castle, it is then attacked by Lord George Murray (1694-1760), Bonnie Prince Charlie's general and the Duke's brother.
1787 Robert Burns (1759-1796), Scotland's iconic poet, visits.
1842 and 1844 Victoria and Albert stay at the castle.
2000's Blair Castle is privately owned. The Dukes of Atholl and Marquises of Tullibardine now live in South Africa.

Blair Castle

Backroads

Clock Tower, Blair Castle

MINGARY CASTLE
8" x 10" oil

**Family / Clan Associations:
MacIan, MacDonald, Campbell**

Nestled upon a rock perch, Mingary Castle serves as the gatekeeper to the Sound of Mull. Parts of the castle date to 1265. Mingary was besieged by rival clans in 1515 and subsequently expanded in the seventeenth and eighteenth centuries. The castle was derelict by 1848. The painting captures the ruin's appearance in 2004.

No Escape

A Legend of Mingary Castle
(Told from the perspective of Abner Pryce)

I stand on Scottish soil, sent here by the English Queen, Elizabeth. I used to keep a diary before I became a spy. Now, an unwritten journal remains trapped within the confines of my head. The words, in peaceful moments, try to escape. My mind is alive with thoughts and stories that, in their telling, could mean my death.

It is October of 1588, and I am warming myself beside a small fire after traveling to the Isle of Mull. I have Mingary Castle directly in view; many other strongholds are visible on the horizon. Speaking with a village girl earlier in the day, I learn that the families from the region are all at war with one another. I find it curious that most kingdoms attack, or defend themselves from other kingdoms; but the Scots seem to prefer battling amongst themselves.

A week ago I witnessed the English destroy most of the Spanish Armada. Traveling from London, I rode two horses to the brink of exhaustion, arriving on distant shores with orders to gather information. Due to horrible weather in the channel, what is left of a shattered Spanish fleet is forced to travel around Scotland. Tomorrow, I will join a fishing party leaving from Tobermory Bay. My mission: to row out into the Atlantic Ocean and make contact with the Spaniards.

By mid-morning, a wounded ship appears on the horizon. The Scottish coastline is treacherous, and our small boat sails out to guide the damaged ship back to harbor. Safely moored, the captain and I exchange a few words. He believes that I am a Scottish fisherman. Some of my new "friends" think that this may be one of Spain's storied galleons, perhaps even *The Florida*, a treasure ship laden with gold and silver. I mention nothing of this, although I know that this is no battleship. In fact, the vessel does not even look Spanish to me; perhaps it is merely one of the boats commandeered for the battle.

The putative *Florida* anchors to procure supplies and make repairs. Her captain demands food and aid from the islanders. News of this ship brings the chief of Clan Maclean, Sir Lachlan, an opportunist, scurrying to make a deal. He requests one-hundred Spanish sailors and two cannons to help him settle a blood-feud with the MacDonalds at Mingary. Provided this agreement is acceptable, the captain can have all the food and aid he likes, as long as he pays for it! Lachlan receives his soldiers; I stay in the bay, making inquiries about other boats with which the "Florida" made contact. The village girl is a wealth of information. I learn that the ship's homeport is Sicily, thus likely to contain troops, but not gold. This piece of information will soon prove problematic when the Spanish captain has nothing to pay Maclean.

I carry on with Shannon, the village girl. Maclean and his newly acquired mercenary army return two days later. They had attacked the MacDonalds on the Isles of Eigg, Muck, Rum and Canna. When MacDonald reinforcements arrived, the Macleans and Spaniards are compelled to withdraw, burning and sacking lands as they are able in their quick retreat.

His ship repaired and supplied, the captain is eager to depart. He announces his desire to sail, and declares that he will only pay Sir Lachlan once his men are returned. Maclean allows the soldiers to board, but keeps three officers hostage. The chief sends a young kinsman, Donald, aboard. By now, the village woman I befriended is whispering to the Maclean chief, her traitorous heart giving away all my secrets. Chief Maclean takes delight in sending an English spy aboard a Spanish ship, a poetic justice. He smiles across at me as we prepare to get underway; I smile back, with a secret of my own: I know that we have been sent to collect a payment that does not exist.

The Spanish captain is quite pleased with himself as well. He pulls up anchor and sets sail, leaving his officers behind. While the ship is still within sight of the coast, the remaining Spaniards are executed by Maclean.

Those on shore watch as the ship sails away. My fear is that in revenge, we will be killed, too. As Donald is led past the powder kegs, he looks over at me and smiles. I ask myself, *why is everyone so jovial?* The clansman then somehow ignites the magazines; the explosion rocks the harbor. Four-hundred feet from shore, everyone aboard the ship is consumed, first by fire, then water. We sink into the depths; and when the grim-reaper smiles, the only response is to smile back. If only for a moment, we cease to be what others have labeled us: captains, maids, and spies. No, we are both kings and jesters who in unison dance on our own graves.

It takes no prophet to predict a spy's death. We regularly meet our end in execution, most often upon betrayal. My demise lacks the pomp and circumstance that I had imagined: this grim reality does not match the prettier picture in my head. Nonetheless, all mortals meet their end. My words and thoughts are free now; from their prior confines within my skull, they have escaped to the printed page. The village girl, as well, is left to tell her stories, passed down in turn through the generations, achieving an immortality of their own. Over 450 years later, beneath the dark blue, almost gray water of the sound, the *Florida* sleeps.

Mingary Castle

1200's A castle of enclosure containing a high curtain wall.
1265 The MacDougalls build the first stone castle.
1493-1495 Mingary is occupied by King James IV (1473-1513) during his campaigns against the MacDonalds.
1499 The lands are granted to Clan MaIain after the MacDougalls oppose the House of Bruce (1306-1371).
1515 Mingary is besieged by the MacDonalds of Lochalsh.
By 1517 The lands of the MacIans were laid waste and the castle is razed.
1519 The Chief of Clan MacIan is killed trying to win back the castle.
1540 The Lands of Ardnamuchan are sold to the Earl of Argyll.
1550's The MaIans support the MacDonalds.
1550's The Maclean of Duart captures the chief of MacIan and unsuccessfully besieged the castle with Spanish soldiers from "The Galleon" in Tobermory Bay. The Campbells take Mingary from the MacIans.
1600 and 1700's Ranges of two-story buildings line the courtyard.
1612 The castle is held by the Campbells.
1644 Mingary is captured by Alasdair Colkitto MacDonald (1610-1647) for the Marquis of Montrose (1612-1650).
1646 The castle is recaptured by the Covenanter General David Leslie (c. 1600-1682).
1651 Mingary Castle is returned to the Campbells of Argyll.
1745 During the Jacobite Rising, the castle is garrisoned for the government (Hanoverians).
By 1848 The castle is inhabitable.
2000's Mingary Castle, privately owned, is a ruin in a dangerous condition.

Sound of Mull

View from the Isle of Mull
9" x 12" oil

DUNVEGAN CASTLE
16" x 20" oil

Family / Clan Associations:
Macleod

From 1270, Dunvegan Castle served as the ancestral home of Clan Macleod. They added a keep in the fourteenth century and constructed additional towers in the sixteenth century. Between 1840 and 1850, the structure was expanded and the original ornamentation removed. During 1938-40, the castle was remodeled again. The painting draws on photos of Dunvegan from 1998.

Intention and Desire

A Legend of Dunvegan Castle

Directly below Dunvegan Castle, a seldom used trail once led to the shore. A small area of underbrush and woodlands occupied the space between the castle and the ocean. Many believed these woods concealed a threshold to another world, an ancient fairy land named Anwan. Those who entered became lost and never returned. If the path was found, then the hair on the back of one's neck would stand. The closer one got to the Cave of the Thresholds, the greater the fear of what it might hold.

An ancient chieftain, Malcolm of the Macleod clan, loved the sea and spent hours listening to the waves crash. The ocean extended past the horizon, then disappeared into the other side. Here he viewed world's edge, studying the earth's curvature and pondering what lay beyond. His thoughts wandered but eventually one question always returned to his mind: *Did he discover new worlds, or did they discover him*?

On his way to watch nature's revelations, he often traveled the path to the shore. Many times he stopped and looked into the cave's darkness where he caught glimpses of a beautiful iridescent light. Through a green mist, there appeared a vision of a young fairy woman. Upon Malcolm's request for her name, she whispered "Ashtanie" as she floated through the air. But she was different from most of her kind, time and again leaving Anwan to observe the one's whose feet were locked to the land. She had a great curiosity; and fairy though she was, she relished human contact.

Malcolm was always mesmerized at her appearing. A glimpse quickly turned to a look, and a smile soon invited words that removed all barriers between them. But once over the threshold, Ashtanie took on human attributes. Her iridescence became skin; her feet touched the earth. When she was with Malcolm, she was as any woman.

The visits between them became more frequent, and the voices calling from beyond sounded more loudly in her ears. Her own kind constantly summoned Ashtanie home. The calls echoed throughout the cave and to escape their reach, Malcolm grabbed Ashtanie's hand and led her far from Anwan.

She spent more and more time away from her world, eventually capturing the notice of her King. Upon return, she was sternly warned not to venture into the earthly world. The King stated, "The only thing that realm offers is a broken heart; your tears will cover all of Scotland, and turn the low-lying ground into lochs." That is, the danger was that Ashtanie's emotions could create a great flood in which the island of Scotland would be engulfed by the sea. Ashtanie relented. But over the course of time, the desires of her heart clouded her reason.

Months passed before her courage grew strong enough to disregard the pragmatism of her King. Ashtanie rushed back to the cave. She was thrilled to find Malcolm standing at the threshold. He had faithfully visited the site looking for Ashtanie. The two continued their courtship; in time Malcolm and Ashtanie became inseparable. She became his wife and bore him a son, who though he had a fairy mother appeared human in all respects.

Ashtanie lived on earth, but missed the land of her own kind. One day Malcolm searched everywhere for his wife before he eventually found her standing at the cave. As her tears fell, so did the rain; and the lochs of Scotland filled to the brim, threatening to overtake the land. Her emotions were magnified in the earthly world, forcing water to flow out of the very rocks. As she turned and looked at Malcolm, he knew that she needed to return to Anwan before the whole land was engulfed. They agreed that she would leave the human realm, and travel back to the mystical land from whence she came.

Malcolm slowly traversed the trail to the castle carrying with him a heavy heart. While everyone dined on venison, duck, and beef, bagpipe music filled the valley. Malcolm paced the corridors of his castle alone, thinking only of Ashtanie. The young girl, assigned to watch over the heir to the Malcolm throne, thought the child asleep, and left him to take part in the celebration. The infant began to cry, with no one to look after him; but Ashtanie heard her son's cries. Unable to bear this, she set out to comfort him.

Flying through the forest in spirit form, she arrived at his side, but was unable to hold him. She remained iridescent; using silk from her scarf to weave a blanket. The fabric's softness on the child's skin, matched with a mother's soothing voice, gave the infant peace. Malcolm was delighted to see his wife one last time. She whispered into his ear the instructions regarding the special blanket. Ashtanie then vanished.

On her return to Anwan, she was brought before the King. She admitted the heart-break he had predicted, but she confessed no regrets. She saw blessing in her love and in her loss. Had she not ventured from her kind, Scotland would have no lochs. Had she stayed with Malcolm her tears would have drowned the nation.

Malcolm lived out his days raising a son who links a clan of this earth to the world beyond. Although he was destined to raise this child alone, many believed his son special, his very presence enabled a time of great prosperity and health for the entire community. Malcolm continued his journeys to the sea. He always looked down Ashtanie's path, but the forest concealed any entry with new growth. Eventually, the cave was lost, the opening either collapsed, or intentionally covered from the other side. Malcolm's and Ashtanie's child grew older, and had little use for a small blanket that looked more like a flag. Malcolm locked it away in an iron case of notable craftsmanship. Only the Chief Macleod was to possess the key.

Throughout the centuries, the waving of the magical flag gave comfort to the clan that occupied the Isle of Skye. Although it was entrusted to Malcolm Macleod, he never used it. Instead, he passed the flag down to the next generation. Many clansmen believe that by the flag, Ashtanie continues watch over the sons and daughters of the island. Whenever the Macleod's are in danger, they can call on its great power.

Horizons, Isle of Skye

Dunvegan Castle

From 1270 The castle is continuously occupied by the Chiefs of Macleod.
1295-1356 Clan Macleod supports King Robert the Bruce (1274-1329) during the Wars of Independence.
1300's A keep rises on what was once an island in Loch Dunvegan.
1411 The Macleods fight at the Battle of Harlaw where Lowland Clans fought the Allies of the Isles (Highland Clans). The battle was indecisive.
1500's The Fairy Tower, a large keep, is built by Alasdair Crotach.
1540 King James V (1512-1542) visits.
1600's An adjoining hall block is added along with another wing.
1650 Clan Macleod supports King Charles II at the Battle of Worcester (1651) that ends in a decisive Cromwell victory. The clan loses five-hundred men, which make them reluctant to take part in the Jacobite Risings.
1745 The Macleods refused to join Bonnie Prince Charlie (1720-1788) unless the Young Pretender had significant military help.
1748 A permanent stone bridge is built across the castle ditch. Dunvegan Castle is now connected to the mainland of Skye.
1840-50 The castle is completely restored and given ornamental turrets.
1847 The Potato Famine strikes Scotland. While other Highland landowners use the famine to clear small tenants from the land, the 25th chief of Clan Macleod bankrupts himself trying to provide for his hungry people. Eventually, he takes a post as a clerk and rents the castle to clear his debts. Later, he is able to return to the castle.
1938-40 The castle is repaired after a fire.
2009 The castle is owned by the 29th Chief of Macleod.

Pastoral Scene, Isle of Skye

DOUNE CASTLE
12" x 9" oil

Royal Castle Associated with the Stewart –Dukes of Albany

Since prehistoric times, a wood fortification has stood on this site located directly above the River Teith. During the fourteenth century, the stone castle that was Doune took shape, serving as a royal hunting lodge, dower house, and prison. The castle suffered devastating sieges in 1645, 1689, and 1715, and was partially restored in 1883. The painting depicts its appearance in 2004.

All Queens and No Kings

A Legend of Doune Castle

An imposing structure towers above the River Tieth: Doune Castle, a royal hunting lodge that belongs to Robert Stewart, the 1st Duke of Albany. The castle is located eight miles outside of Stirling, an important political center of Scotland.

Much as fifteenth century life entails a struggle to survive, a departure from the well-established routine on which castle life turns brings welcome relief. The job of disrupting the monotony needs someone with a free rein on speech, the liberty to say what others should not or cannot. It falls to uncommon, occasionally mad, itinerant actors, whose appearances around Scotland are rare, and so awaited with great anticipation.

One such unkempt fool, a Jester, arrives at Doune Castle, at the Duke's own invitation. He stands in the center of the castle courtyard wearing his brightly colored clothes. Atop his head is a floppy hat ending in three points, representative of a donkey's ears and tail. Each point has a jingling bell attached to the end, which rings with every step. Carrying a mock scepter, he pokes royal jest at everyone. Soon the cheers and laughter of those he entertains echo through the Great Hall of Doune Castle, the Jester's own laughter, too. Yet, what's truly extraordinary about this Jester is that he claims to see the future.

After the entertainment, Robert Stewart withdraws to the Duke's Hall, the Jester accompanying him. Removing his costume, he challenges Robert to a game of cards. As skilled as both players are rumored to be, the Jester wins round after round. Growing bored, he agrees to one last hand, referring to it as 'the prophecy round.' Both men take their time, studying each other for long stretches. Pleased with what he sees, the Duke calls the hand. The Jester puts down three Queens and two Nines of Diamonds – yes, two! It seems as though he has had some extra cards up his loose sleeves, which, if nothing else, calls his earlier victories into question.

Firebasket, Great Hall

The Duke's Hall

"Another winning hand!" the Jester nonetheless declares. Standing up and pointing to his cards, he adds, "The Curse of Scotland!" Then, donning his ass's hat, he dances toward the door. When the Duke accosts him before he can leave, demanding an explanation of the curse, the Jester smiles widely and answers, "It's in the cards: three queens and two crosses." Used to hearing such opaque things from the Jester, Robert shrugs his shoulders, shakes his head, and lets the conversation end.

For years after the Jester's visit, Robert would remember and reflect on the game of cards. Recalling the game's outcome, he would counsel, "Never play cards with a fool – a natural fool, simple by nature, or a professional fool, whose folly enjoys the protection of the crown; either way it ends badly for everyone." He would often add, "There seem to be two kinds of prophets, too – one accidental, happening on the truth by luck, and the other cryptic, truly intuiting the divine. In any event, time bears out all truths, and all falsehoods."

***

After that same Duke of Albany died in 1420, Doune Castle began its long career as a dower house, or residence of widows. The first of them, in 1460, was Mary Gueldres, widowed after King James II was killed by one of his own cannons at Roxburgh. Next was Margaret of Denmark, married to James III, who was killed at the Battle of Sauchieburn. The last was Margaret Tudor, married to James IV, who lost his life at the Battle of Flodden. It unfolded, then, just as the Jester predicted – three queens, all widowed one after the other.

Not to forget the Nine of Diamonds: it has long held native claim to being the 'Curse of Scotland.' The word *curse* likely represents a corruption of *cross*, because the Nine's diamonds are arranged in the shape of a St. Andrew's Cross. And the card has turned up, strangely, in a number of Scottish disasters. The disposition of forces on the Flodden battlefield was drawn up on a Nine of Diamonds; the orders for the Massacre of Glencoe in 1692 were likewise signed on the back of a Nine of Diamonds. So this Jester: was he an 'accidental' or a 'cryptic' prophet?

Doune Castle

1300's Doune Castle consists of two strong towers connected to a lower range built by Robert Stewart, Duke of Albany (c. 1340- 1420). He virtually rules Scotland during the reign of Robert III (c. 1340-1406).
Until 1570 Doune is occasionally used by Mary, Queen of Scots (1542-1587), and held by forces loyal to her.
1645 Doune is occupied by the Marquis of Montrose (1612-1650).
1689 and 1715 Doune Castle is occupied by Government (Hanoverian) troops.
1745 Taken by Jacobite troops and used as a prison. The castle is entrusted to the governorship of MacGregor of Glengyle.
1746 After the Jacobite victory at Falkirk, Doune housed many prisoners including the young Rev. John Witherspoon (1723-1794), later the architect of the American Declaration of Independence (1776).
1800's The castle is derelict. In 1883, the Earl of Moray restores Doune replacing the timber roofs and interior floors.
2000's Doune is managed by Historic Scotland. This unique castle was originally completed in a single building period and has survived relatively unchanged and complete.

Doune Castle

KILRAVOCK CASTLE
8" x 10" oil

**Family / Clan Associations:
Bisset and Rose**

Kilravock Castle is believed to be built over the site of an ancient Christian chapel. An early keep dates to the fifteenth century. The castle was expanded in the sixteenth century, with the keep being extended and fortified in the seventeenth century. Further construction occurred in 1730. The painting depicts Kilravock's appearance in 2007.

Always Welcome

A Legend of Kilravock Castle

A canopy of trees lines the path to a Highlands sanctuary. Kilravock Castle stands in a haven of forests, hills, valleys, and small lochs, all which invite exploration. Heart-shaped branches, a gooseberry bush growing above the earth, and the River Nairn can all be discovered near the structure. *Kil* is the Celtic word for church with the present castle built on the site of ancient chapel where St. Columba preached in 565.

Falling Leaves

The Roses are considered a leading family of the Highlands. They welcome all, honoring centuries of tradition regarding Kilravock as a place of refuge The first Roses entered Scotland in the early thirteenth century and lived in a house located upon a nearby hill. The central tower of the present castle was completed by 1460; further expansion occurs throughout the centuries. The 10th Laird added the south wing in 1553 to house seventeen female dependents. The castle boasts the usual who's who list of visitors: Mary Queen of Scots in 1562, her son James VI in 1589. The latter inquired into the Laird's diplomatic skills, living amongst such violent neighbors. The Laird famously replied, "They are the best neighbors I could have, for they make me go to God upon my knees thrice a day, when perhaps otherwise I would not have gone once." He lived to be ninety!

The Roses were Covenanters (Presbyterian) and provided sanctuary for all those in need during the troubled religious periods which preceded the Glorious Revolution of 1688. The 15th Laird, a member of Scottish Parliament, voted against the union with England in 1707. In the first Jacobite uprising of 1715, he raised two-hundred of his clan members to preserve the peace in the area. He garrisoned the castle against the Jacobites. Later, he joined forces with Lord Lovat of the Frasers, and Clan Grant. Together, they successfully besieged nearby Inverness, which was being held by the Jacobite Sir John Mackenzie of Coul. In the days before the Battle of Culloden, the family hosted the Jacobite commander, Bonnie Prince Charlie. One day later they welcomed the opposing commander, the Duke of Cumberland.

Throughout turbulent times, those on both sides of any issue have stepped across the welcome mat that defines Kilravock Castle. Earlier in the 1700's,

Robert Burns, the iconic Scottish poet, composed a poem under the castle's most famous tree, notable for its heart-shaped branches. From the 1800's on, Kilravock and the Roses enjoy a time of peace.

In the setting of gardens and woodlands, a heartfelt reception greets all who visit this continually inhabited castle. The keep's walls are eight feet thick and provide protection both then and now. The castle is a symbol in itself, but perhaps the most powerful icon is the gooseberry bush growing from the top of the old tower. Legend states that as long as the bush grows, a member of the Rose family will inhabit the castle. Recently the bush began to wither; so Ms. Elizabeth Rose, the 25th Baroness, planted another, which is reported to be thriving! The castle presently operates as a Christian center, carrying on the family traditions.

Kilravock Castle
(Pronounced Kilrawk)

After the 500's The first six generations of the Rose family lived in a house at the top of a hill by the Cedar of Lebanon tree.
1460 The Baron of Kilravock was granted a license to build by the Lord of the Isles. A massive keep of five stories is constructed.
1553 A mansion house is added to accommodate a household of seventeen female dependents.
1562 Mary, Queen of Scots (1542-1587) visits the castle.
1600's The keep is extended, and in 1730 a main entrance and stairway is added.
1926 A scullery, pantry, and bathroom were built.
From 1967 The castle is managed by the Kilravock Christian Trust.
2000's The castle has been continuously occupied since 1460 and currently operates as a bed and breakfast accommodation.

Old Man of Storr 8" x 10" oil

Glenfinnan Monument 9" x 12" oil

Heart-Shaped Branches 8" x 10" oil

CASTLE STALKER
8" x 10" oil

**Family / Clan Associations:
Stewart of Appin and Campbell**

Castle Stalker sits on the Rock of the Cormorants, an islet in Loch Laich reachable only by boat. The castle was built in 1388 for use as hunting lodge; it was remodeled in the sixteenth century. In 1745 the castle was unsuccessfully besieged by the Jacobites, their two-pound cannon balls bouncing off the thick walls. Eventually falling into dereliction, Stalker was abandoned by 1780 and in ruins after 1831; it was restored in the 1960's. The painting draws on a 2004 view.

Symbols of Strength

A Legend of Castle Stalker

It is 1520, an ordinary day in Scotland. Notable perhaps for the rare morning sunshine that has now turned to gloom, clouds cover the sky and mist hangs in the air. As a storm moves across the water, a marauding Campbell party overtakes Alexander Stewart who is fishing off an isle in Loch Laich. The ground, near the fortress of Castle Stalker, is stained red with Stewart blood. Clan Campbell then ransacks the castle. But they are unaware that Alexander's infant son, Donald Stewart, has been hidden by his nurse in the refuge of a secret room. To keep the infant quiet, she rocks the child singing in a whisper. The two go unnoticed. The Campbells quickly pillage the castle and vanish into the mist.

The nurse and Donald flee from the western seaboard of Scotland while traveling to the hills of Caithness and take refuge in Morvin, a mythical Gaelic Kingdom. The years pass and Donald grows into a large man, revered as a symbol of strength. He earns his reputation as a great warrior, and his name, Donald the Hammer, due to his ability to simultaneously swing two blacksmith's hammers in battle.

Back on the small island of his father's death, the storms from the sea still enter quickly and exit gracefully on the wind. In the midst of such a storm, Donald returns. The commotion surrounds him, rain covers his face, he listens for his father's voice, and he hears no words only the cries of his father's blood. Madness overtakes the warrior; he vows revenge as he departs the island.

Death for death is the prevailing justice. By 1544, Donald has raised the Stewarts of Appin to do unto the Campbells as they had done to the Stewarts. A raiding party travels to nearby Dunstaffnage Castle and kills nine Campbell clansmen. Donald later leads the Stewarts (to defeat) at the Battle of Pinkie Cleugh near the River Esk in September of 1547. Donald then enters a more peaceful stage of his life. He dies in 1607 and is buried on the Isle of Lismore.

In 1620, Castle Stalker passes to Clan Campbell, in exchange for an 'eight-oared' wherry, as the outcome of the 7th Stewart chief Duncan's drunken wager. In 1745, fifty-nine Campbells hold out against a siege of three-hundred Stewarts faithful to the Jacobites. Two pound cannon balls bounce off the walls. The castle is later used to re-supply troops, and becomes an integral in the success of government forces that defeat the Jacobite cause.

Castle Stalker

1300's The first castle is built by the MacDougall Lords of Lorn.
1338 Castle Stalker, much in its present form, is built by Duncan Stewart of Appin.
c. 1500 Castle Stalker is used by King James IV (1473-1513) as a hunting lodge.
1620 The castle is sold to the Campbells. Local tradition states the 7th Stewart laird drunkenly wagers the castle in exchange for an eight oared wherry.
1685 The Stewarts regain the castle after a long siege.
1715 Clan Stewart fought for the Jacobites at The Battle of Sheriffmuir where British Government forces achieved victory over Jacobite Rebels.
1745 Three-hundred Appin Clansmen besieged Castle Stalker against a Campbell garrison of sixty men. They fail to take Stalker, a heavy loss for the Jacobite cause. The castle becomes an important stop on the supply route between Inverary and Fort William.
1765 The estate is sold, although by 1780 the castle is abandoned. After **1831**, the Castle is roofless.
1960's The castle is restored.
2000's Castle Stalker is privately owned.

Castle Stalker

KILCHURN CASTLE
9" x 12" oil

Family / Clan Associations:
MacGregor and Campbell of Glenorchy

Located on a small island at the head of Loch Awe, Kilchurn Castle dates to 1440. In the years after 1500, Kilchurn became a key link in the chain of castles sustaining Campbell power in Western Scotland. The structure saw expansion through the sixteenth century and three corner towers added in the late seventeenth century. Kilchurn was besieged in 1654, was abandoned by 1740, and lost its roof in 1745. The painting depicts a 2004 view.

Keystones of the Realm

A Legend of Kilchurn Castle

It is the mid 1400's, and Kilchurn Castle, the monument of Loch Awe, is being built by Clan Campbell on an island previously owned by Clan MacGregor. Sir Colin Campbell begins the construction of Kilchurn but soon travels to Rome to take part in Crusading exploits. While there, he earns the name, *Black Knight of Rhodes*. He does not return to Scotland until after the castle's completion leaving oversight responsibilities to his wife Margaret.

Many onlookers gather in anticipation as the basement vault of Kilchurn is being finished. The great stone ribs span the ceiling from the walls. But would they carry the load above when the wooden beams that now bear the weight are removed. Like a reverse puzzle, piece by piece, the scaffolding is disassembled. Per tradition, the master mason stands in the center of the recently completed basement. He directs as each support is removed. Life or death hangs on the quality of construction, and if the room is properly built, it supports the structure above. Otherwise the weight of the building will come down, crushing the mason who serves as both architect and builder. Standing with hands at his side, he broadcasts a confident smile. As the last supporting board is removed, a hush falls. Then Margaret Campbell begins clapping to the shouts to all. The room is complete, the mason alive, and the building is prepared to withstand sieges and reconstructions through the centuries.

Kilchurn Castle
(Pronounced Killhern)

1300's The lands are originally held by the MacGregors, who had a stronghold on the small island. The property was acquired by the Campbells of Glenorchy.
1440 A courtyard castle is built by Sir Colin Campbell of Glenorchy. It consists of a rectangular keep of four stories.
1500's Damage, inflicted by the MacGregors, is repaired.
1500 and 1600's A range of buildings is added.
1600's Barrack blocks and two large kitchens are added.
1654 Kilchurn is besieged by Royalists under General Middleton until relieved by Cromwellian forces sent by Monck.
1685 Kilchurn is besieged by the Protestant Earl of Argyll when he rebels against the Catholic King James VII (1633-1701).
1690 Sir John Campbell, 1st Earl of Breadalbane (1636-1717) builds a barracks block capable of holding over 200 troops.
1715 and 1745 Kilchurn is garrisoned with Hanoverian redcoats during the Jacobite Risings.
Until 1740 The castle is inhabited by the Campbells. After 1740, they move to Ballach, which is now known as Taymouth.
1745 The castle is garrisoned by Hanoverian troops.
By **1775** Kilchurn is unroofed.
1817 Drainage work on the outflow from the Loch Awe lowers the waters. Once the castle entirely covered the small island linked to the shore by a secret causeway hidden below the surface of the water.
2000's The castle is undergoing some restoration and is under the guidance of Historic Scotland.

Oban, Scotland

Mist over Loch Awe

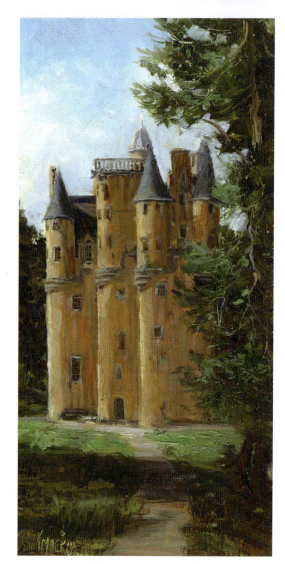

CRAIGIEVAR CASTLE
12"x6" oil

**Family / Clan Associations:
Mortimer and Forbes**

Craigievar Castle was constructed in 1626 by the Mortimer's, but after their bankruptcy, the Forbes family purchased and completed the house. Craigievar castle underwent repair in 1823. The painting is based on a visit in 2004.

Partnerships

A Legend of Craigievar Castle

One finds tower houses throughout Scotland, but Craigievar Castle near Alford bids well to being the finest. Craigievar was among the last of its type built. The house, begun by the Mortimers, quickly bankrupted them. William Forbes, better known as Danzig *Willie*, was the next to purchase the estate. Forbes was a rich merchant from Aberdeen, who made his fortune in the lands surrounding the Baltic Sea. Willie marketed fish and woolen goods from Scotland to the cities of Germany; timber made the return trip. Between 1610 and 1627, *Willie* invested the proceeds of this flourishing trade in Craigievar's completion. He employed a master mason, John Bell, and the resulting partnership proved highly successful. Sadly, Forbes only enjoyed his house for a year, dying in 1627.

Craigievar Castle

1457 The property is named after a nearby hill, and initially belongs to the Mortimers. They hold it until 1610. Upon bankruptcy, the castle is sold to the Forbes family.

1626 The castle is completed by the Forbes of Menie.

1823 Sir John Forbes, the 7th Baronet restores the castle, without amendment, to the original vision. This represents one of the earliest cases of preserving a building for its aesthetic and historic value.

1914-1918 During World War I, the castle is used as a hospital for wounded Belgian soldiers.

1963 The castle is entrusted to the state. Craigievar is a fine example of Scottish Baronial Architecture, and is known for its plasterwork ceilings.

2006 The castle, its estate, over two-hundred acres of farms and woodlands are owned and managed by the National Trust of Scotland.

The view from Craigievar

Craigievar Castle

BRAEMAR CASTLE
8" x 10" oil

Family / Clan Associations:
Erskine and Farquharson

Braemar Castle began in 1628 as a hunting lodge. The structure was badly burned in the first Jacobite uprising of 1689, losing its roof by 1715. That same year, the Earl of Mar raised the standard of James VIII and III upon a small hill near the village of Braemar, marking the beginning of the second Jacobite uprising. By 1748 Braemar castle was derelict; but it was eventually restored by the Hanoverian government, who commissioned John Adams, Scotland's famous architect, to repair the upper floors. The painting depicts a 2006 vantage.

Gatherings

A Legend of Braemar Castle
(Told from the perspective of Restorious)

I am Restorius, the grandest fairy in our secret village, located in the Forest of Mar, a dark, uninviting haunt. Centuries ago, some humans – they called themselves 'Romans' – named its pine, juniper, birch, and hazel *the Great Forest of Caledon*. The trees are as tall as twenty fairies, head to toe, and the undergrowth is forbidding. In places, one can barely see into it. Yet, the forest grants entry to those who know the terrain; and from our sanctuary there, we survey the world, teeming with life and prosperity, of the tall-ones traversing the Highlands crossroads before our eyes.

We have been observing these humans for generations, in fact, documenting their events, and occasionally even mimicking their ways. Frankly, these tall-ones all look the same to us – in contrast to us fairies, each so distinct, no two of us alike. They are so fragile, too, subject to all sorts of maladies and treacheries, and cycle swiftly through birth and death. We fairies, in contrast, live through the ages, outside of time.

Ordinarily, that is. In a rare twist – a first for me – our community just held a funeral, and for a fairy named Eternity, no less. Several of us had witnessed his end. He was amongst the tall-ones, on the field of celebration during their Games, when a boulder from the hammer toss landed on his head. Clearly dazed, he stumbled dizzily for a moment, capsized, and never recovered. Circling, we all poked and kicked him, to no avail. I dug a hole for his little fairy body; but before we could throw him in, he turned to dust and was carried off on the wind. With no corpse to commit to the earth, our service ended abruptly.

Before we scattered, however, my comrades put Eternity's coat on me. (It's a dull brown, and I prefer the lively green of my own skin. I shall have to clean it immediately; we fairies are creatures of impeccable polish, standing proud and shining in the sun.) Knowing how fairies collect things, I quickly explored what I'd inherited: the right pocket contained a tooth, arm bone, kneecap, and some fingers, while the left held a dusty book, *The Chronicles*. Right there, atop Kenneth's Hill – where the Highland Games that the tall-ones love, and for which they still congregate, began over a thousand years ago – I showed my comrades the important contents.

You see, most fairies live to make mischief, our large smiles and appearance of innocence notwithstanding. That would have been my vocation, too, had Eternity lived and had I not inherited his coat. But, fairy tradition dictates that the possessor of the coat and caretaker of the bones becomes the Chronicler of the ages. Thus, I had been given, with Eternity's coat, a commission: to keep and tell the great stories – tales without beginning or end, as immemorial as time itself – until I hand them on to another, as faithfully as Eternity and his predecessors had entrusted them to me.

Sitting now in the deep recesses of the forest, I read. I can't help wondering why these humans cannot see us. "What's wrong with their eyes?" I ask. Then I come to the story of St. Rule, who saw so much with unique clarity; and I finger, with fresh insight, what's in my pocket – the very bones of St. Andrew, the Galilean fisherman and apostle of Christ! – as I read:

…St. Rule, or Regulus as he prefers to be called, is warned in a dream that the remains of St. Andrew need to be moved to the ends of the earth for safe-keeping. As instructed by the angel, St. Rule removes a few bones from St. Andrews tomb and begins his journey. After arriving shipwrecked on the rocky Scottish coast, he travels inland with his treasure to the village of Doldencha. It's there that I, Eternity, befriend him. His treasure, these bones of St. Andrew that have such magical and life-saving power, is much sought after by the tall ones. The bones are the occasion of our first interaction with humans.

...St. Rule establishes a church here in Braemar; first known as the Parish of St. Andrew, it later is called Kindrochit. Then he travels to what is now St. Andrews and has a tower built next to Scotland's largest cathedral. For an unrecorded time, the bones of Scotland's Patron Saint are displayed in that grand cathedral overlooking the coast. Upon its destruction in 1559, we fairies recover the bones...

They've been in our care for over five-hundred years, I realize! I skip a couple of pages ahead:

...Three-hundred years after St. Rule, in 1060, a Pictish King, a man they call Malcolm Canmore, and his Queen come to Braemar. He holds a gathering, or what the tall ones call 'Highland Games,' awarding prizes for feats of strength and skill that serve to select the ablest warriors. From then on, the celebrations take place once a year in autumn. We fairies look forward to them, too, developing our own traditions around them...

Valley near Braemar Castle

The chronicler moves on:

...The tall ones use their great strength, perhaps enhanced through the Games, to build a stone structure. They name it Kindrochit Castle. It becomes a hunting lodge, from which the great hunts that preceded the Games are hosted. From 1057 to 1093, many "colorful ones" – Scottish royalty – visit and take part. The tall-ones also build a wooden bridge across the River Clunie, which flows through the center of Braemar. It's the only crossing for several miles. We fairies use the bridge, too, after bathing in the river, and sometimes travel across it to dance on the tops of other hills...

I put the book back in my pocket and ponder how we fairies live in trees, while the tall-ones stack stone orderly to make living space. I remember when the tall-ones busied themselves, in 1628, building a new structure. They named it Braemar Castle. Many of our songs are about the fortress – we are in awe of it! Being barely able to lift a rock, we think constructing a castle an achievement, indeed!

After a nap, I return to *The Chronicles*, reading about a special event in 1715:

...One of the most memorable gatherings takes place when a leader of the tall-ones, John Erskine, 24th Earl of Mar, summons about two-thousand Highlanders to a ceremony called 'The Raising of the Standard for a Rally to Prince Charlie's Banner.' I watch, incredulous, as, on a small hill in Braemar, they lift a small piece of cloth – a 'flag,' they call it – into the sky. Something apparently goes wrong: the ball on top of their flagpole detaches as the flag ascends, and ball, flag, and rope fall to the ground. It's an omen of disaster, I learn some thirty years afterwards, when most of these men are slaughtered at their Battle of Culloden...

I *know* that flagpole ball, I realize; we fairies have it hidden in the forest!

Reading on, I am interested to note that, in the years following 1746, the chronicler's annual entries record that no Games were held, and that the larger tall-ones no longer wore their tartan dress. Men from another land, it seems, have prohibited the tall-ones from celebrating their heritage. The fairies continue to assemble, but the gatherings of the tall-ones do not resume until 1782. I see a note in the margin that reads: "The men from the far-away land repealed their act." I relish recalling that, from then on, the Games grow steadily in numbers and are well-established by 1800.

I paraphrase aloud some of the history for comrades who've come near. I tell them about the pomp and circumstance of 1826, when the tall-ones first organized themselves into what they call the 'Highland Society.' They especially enjoy hearing the chronicler's report, in the entry about the first modern Games in 1832, which "the tall-ones begin to pass valuable paper coupons back and forth." We laugh because these 'notes' are highly coveted still – which is why we fairies dedicate whole days to stealing them, a custom that continues to this day. We tear them into scraps and use them at night to kindle our hilltop fires, and dance beneath the starlit sky.

I press on to relate how highly structured the Games have become. My comrades love hearing about all the activities that revolve around the tall-ones throwing things, mainly rocks and trees, and – later at night – each other. We marvel together at a thousand years of throwing things!

I take a breath. Then I tell of the frequent appearance, beginning in 1848, of the decorated and celebrated ones, wearing bright colors, adorned with shiny stones, and bearing special titles: Kings and Queens. We laugh, again, to recall how Eternity, taking a page from the tall-ones, organized a committee to determine how best to transfer possession of the precious jewels from them to us. We know how many 'pretties' the tall-ones will never recover, because they're hidden in the trees.

I close with the account of how, in 1906, the Duke of Fife bequeathed twelve acres of the Mar Estate to the Braemar Highland Society, providing the site for the current Braemar Games. Then, when my comrades drift off to watch what the tall-ones are up to, I decide to try my first written entry:

…It is September and the valley is filled with humanity. Probably twenty-thousand tall-ones are here. Some spin around, throw rocks, hurl trees; at times, they follow right after one another, copying the other's motions. All are brightly attired. Many exchange paper coupons and drink brown water out of miniature glasses. Bladder-shaped, horned instruments shriek continually, and the whole affair smells of the unwashed.

My comrades and I look forward to this every year. We compete, too – to see who can collect the greatest number of shiny things. Often, fairies from the other valleys join us. We have a prize for the one who can cause the most trouble, steal the most valuables, remove the most tent-stakes. He or she has the honor of starting the fire each night, before which we dance in celebration.

As the closing ceremonies adjourn, the humans march away, and the fairies disappear into the forest, I wonder if Eternity's death has changed things forever, if it has marked the beginning of time for us. Will we fairies now have a different outlook on life? Will we, too, rush

Clunie River

anxiously about, knowing that it is possible for us no longer to exist? I begin to understand the ways of the tall-ones – their hopes and fears. I sense what a curious thing time is, adding a certain urgency to everything. I feel a sudden desire to return that which we have taken. What if we restored the ball to the top of the flagpole? What if I traveled to St. Andrews and placed the revered bones of the apostle back in their proper place? I dare to imagine all the shiny things, which we fairies have traded back and forth for centuries, left at the feet of these humans during next year's celebration. Well, all of them, maybe, but my favorite shiny tent-stake.
~ Restorius

Braemar Castle

1628 The Castle is built by John Erskine, Earl of Mar.
1689 Braemar is captured and burned by John Farquharson of Inverey, The Black Colonel.
Until 1748 The castle is in ruin.
1715 John, 11th Earl of Mar (1675-1732), led the 1715 Jacobite Rising. The Earl raised the Royal Standard of James VIII (1688-1776) The Old Pretender on a small hill in the village of Braemar.
1715 The Mar is stripped of his lands and forced into exile after the Battle of Sheriffmuir where British Government forces achieved victory over Jacobite Rebels.
1732 The property passes to the Farquharsons of Invercauld.
After 1746 The castle is taken over by the government, refurbished and transformed into barracks.
1797 The troops leave.
1800's The castle is restored and reoccupied by the Farquharsons. Queen Victoria (1819-1901) visits when attending the Braemar Games.
2000's Braemar Castle is privately owned.

The view from Braemar Village

Braemar Castle

Stirling Castle
9" x 12" oil
The Highlands

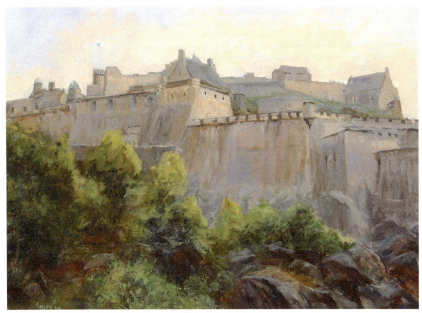

Edinburgh Castle
20" x 24" oil
The Lowlands

THE LOWLANDS

Scotland, taken in its entirety, can be understood as an amalgamation of region and culture. Throughout the centuries, families and noble houses have always been more prominent to the Lowlands. However, any description of indigenous Scots is based upon kinship identity. In addition to the native Scots, those of Scottish ancestry claim distinct heritage and origin.

The Highland Boundary Line should not be viewed as definitive. The Highlands or Lowlands are not official geographical regions of Scotland. There are areas of the "Lowlands," such as the Southern Uplands that reach to 2,765 feet, although many of the islands exist at sea level.

The Lowlands as a term can be defined by cultural influences. The Celtic inhabitants of ancient Alba (Gaelic name for Scotland) were made up of diverse tribes, which in the south were comprised of Anglo-Saxons, Britons, and Normans. In addition to the tribes, Roman incursions into the land they called Caledonia occurred from around 71 until their exit from Britannia in 213. The Romans began construction of Hadrian's Wall in 122. The wall is located in the southern reaches of the kingdom near the present border between Scotland and England. Further north, another Roman wall, named Antonine's Wall, was constructed twenty years later in 142. This wall spans the distance between the Firth of Clyde and the Firth of Forth.

By 654, the Kingdom of Northumbria (made up of the Angles) existed in northwest England and southern Scotland. The Kingdom of Scotland dates to 843 when the first Scottish King, Kenneth MacAlpine, united the Scots and the Picts. This Kingdom existed as an independent state until 1707 and occupied the northern third of the island of Great Britain. Since 1482, following England's control of Berwick (a coastal town located on the border), the territory of the Kingdom of Scotland corresponded to that of modern day Scotland. From 1707, the Kingdoms of Scotland and England were united to form Great Britain. This occurred under the Act of Union.

Scotland, past and present, occupies an area bounded by the North Sea to the east, the Atlantic Ocean to the north and west, and the Irish Sea to the southwest. Apart from the mainland, Scotland consists of over seven-hundred small islands.

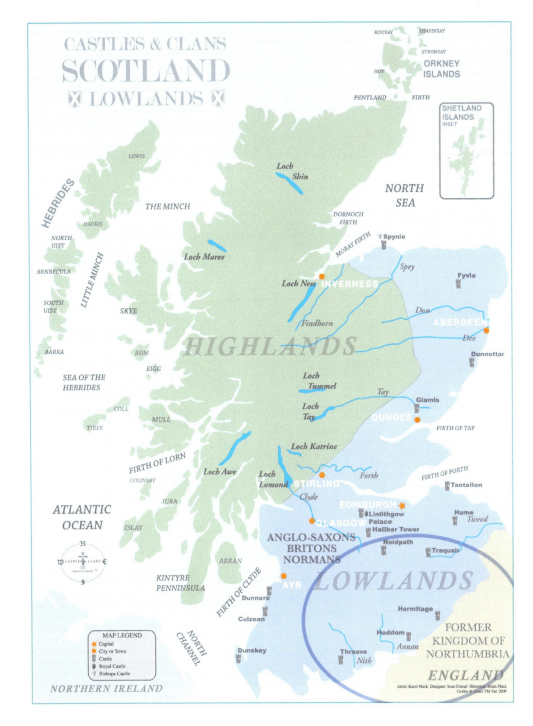

Towards the Sky

The Back Country

Dunure Harbor

Wind Through the trees, Scottish Lowlands

Corra Linn - Falls of Clyde 16" x 12" oil

Grey Mare's Tail 20" x 8" oil

Courtyard Cottages 8" x 10" oil

THREAVE CASTLE
8" x 10" oil

**Family / Clan Associations:
Douglas, Maxwell, and Gordon**

Threave Castle sits on an island in the River Dee, which originally was the site of a small village that could only be approached by boat. The first fortress at Threave was erected as a royal retreat in the twelfth century it was destroyed in 1308. A new keep arose in 1369, augmented by expansion and fortification in 1447. Much of what remains today dates from this era. The castle was besieged in 1455, and again in 1640, after which the structure was abandoned and fell into ruin. The painting is based on a 2006 view.

Wizards of Intuition

A Legend of Threave Castle
(Told from the perspective of Malcolm and Elizabeth Fleming)

Cold damp air fills my lungs, the breath of life visible upon exhale. There is a peace here, ten stories above the earth. Surrounded by silence, I hear my own heartbeat. High above the blacksmiths, carpenters, and cooks, life could be lived uninterrupted. As part of my routine, I climb the additional stairs leading to the battlements of Threave Castle. From this vantage, I have seen as seasons unfold, nature's extremes of harmony and chaos in impressive display. Before this day and the next four end, I will experience extremes no less wild.

Storms, like the one before me, come and go in the borders of Scotland. With thick clouds concealing the sun, the sudden flash of brilliant red and yellow – colors of a royal messenger – pierces the overcast landscape. Agents of change inevitably appear on this horizon first, then find their way to the castle gates before they disturb our lives.

A sentry inquires about the rider, "Is he royalty?"

"Aye, and no ordinary royalty, but from the King's court," I reply.

The sentry jokingly continues, "Has he come to surrender the crown?"

We share a laugh that ends quickly. There is a seriousness surrounding a message from the King.

My name carries through the keep, "Sir Malcolm Fleming!" Although I am advisor to the 6th Earl, that lofty title never crosses the lips of my wife Elizabeth. Instead, she humbles, referring to me with a mock nobility, as the *Wizard of Intuition*. In any case, it is I who am summoned to offer counsel to William Douglas, the Earl, on this 23rd day of November, 1440. A clerk appears, bows and states, "Sir Malcolm, your presence is required in the Great Hall." Forcing a smile, I respond, "I am sure it is."

I linger a few moments to catch a glimpse of Elizabeth. Far below, she is walking towards the keep to oversee preparation of the evening meal. She has a grace and beauty desired by others, and she is a much more social creature than I. Her daily duties allow her access to many individuals - and to what they know - which lends considerable assistance to my work as advisor. The information she gleans often proves more useful than that received from my official sources. Retaining thoughts of my Elizabeth, I descend to the Earl's chambers.

There is always a draft in the circular stone stairway that sends a chill through my body. I meet the messenger on a landing; he mumbles his name. I believe he says, "Edward," but I am not sure. Nor, do I have much interest: messengers often lose their heads! If this man remains alive, then I will speak with him. Edward hands me the scroll, and I enter the Great Hall, which is sparsely populated. The Chaplin, the Earl, and a few others are already seated and engaged in discussion; their voices echo within the immense room. I bide my time listening and warming myself by the fire; soon enough, I will add my own words to the confusion of voices.

My first order of business is to authenticate the message. The elaborately carved crests, of all the surrounding families of Scotland's royalty, are widely used as ceiling decorations; but that is not their primary purpose. I verify the seal pressed into the wax, embossed by the King's signet ring; there are no signs of tampering. I hand the scroll to the Earl, stating, "It is authentic, my lord." I retreat back into the stairway to speak with Edward. My suspicions already aroused, I notice that he is large for a messenger, a characteristic that disturbs me. Messengers are normally diminutives, so as not to tire the horses.

For some time, I stare at Edward waiting on his words. He stands before me steady as a statue, granting me nothing save silence. I launch my inquiry, "By what authority do you enter Threave Castle?"

"That of the King of Scotland, James II," Edward replies.

"Yes, and what is your commission?"

"Sir, I am a messenger." I think to myself: *a man of few words, who states the obvious; perhaps he is a simple creature of task.* After a long lull in the conversation, his voice breaks the silence, "I serve Scotland."

"Edward, what if I told you the scroll ordered your execution?"

He quickly drops to one knee, "I serve the crown." His words are a subtle reminder to me regarding the value of his life. Those whom serve the crown are accounted for and will be missed. He continues in a soft voice, "I am a simple man my lord."

"I am not your lord; rise Edward." I look up, staring into his eyes, "You present to me one face, but I wonder if you are concealing another?"

Edward replies, "I am the man that stands before you, Sir." Although I dismiss him, I am not convinced that he is telling the truth.

Elizabeth meets me in the stairway, displaying an agitation that distracts from her beauty. Grabbing me by the arm, she states, "I have news." It is distracting to be this close to her. With renewed effort, I focus my attention on official matters of the realm. She tightens her grip, exclaiming "Listen! those in Edinburgh view the powers in the south of Scotland as a threat. Especially the Douglas family. The message comes from Livingston and Crichton, advisors to the young King."

I ask, "What is the message?"

"An invitation to the Earl and his brother to a dinner of reconciliation. Use caution Malcolm; I will see what else I can find out. I fear this is not good news, and nothing is what it seems in this King's court. Be off with you now."

"Anything else?"

"No, no," She smiles and pushes me away.

As usual, we gather in the Great Hall for dinner. This evening, all the advisors are present. I remember why I dread these affairs: everyone talking at once, proposing their grandiose schemes, often, rarely discoursing on the subject at hand. For all that is accomplished, we may as well gather a group of dogs and listen to them bark. Woodring, the constable, is sitting across from me, a man barely tolerable for his stench alone. The hair atop his head is alive with lice. Mumbling, he runs his words together; even if I wanted to, I cannot understand him. On top of such oddities, the constable is obese; and he always makes a point of showing others his belly, clutching his fat with both hands and exclaiming, "Good food!" As if his blubber were a sign of stature and wealth! I feel a fresh urge to press the Earl about replacing Woodring, emphasizing how poorly this uncouth savage reflects on his office as Earl. No doubt, the Earl will ignore my advice, again arguing, "He is a man who gets things done, and everybody needs one of those." I won't be able to disagree, even if I find Woodring's practices and person loathsome. All this aside, I am confident that, following the mindless chatter, the Earl will speak with me alone. I bide my time until then.

The dinner concludes as servants bring dessert. The Earl's younger brother David is in attendance and reads the King's invitation aloud:

The Edge of the Wilderness

His majesty, King James II,
Invites the 6th Earl of Douglas and David Douglas
to attend a dinner of reconciliation.
Their presence requested the 24th day of November.
The Great Hall of Edinburgh Castle.

Much discussion follows regarding the Earl's and David's attendance. I fear the outcome will have us traveling the next day. The young Earl is eager to appear before the court. He views it as an opportunity to strengthen his alliance with the King.

Once the others depart, I am left to counsel the Earl. He wishes to know my thoughts regarding the invitation. I oblige "I think it unwise to leave this castle." I tell him, "Send word that the demands of your office do not allow your attendance. William, your power is solidified in the south; a man can be content with a kingdom such as this."

My attempts at curbing his youthful enthusiasm fail. He laughs, "Oh yes, Malcolm, a castle and lands such as these, but do not forget that it is the King who grants me this kingdom. And, if this King requests my presence, my presence he will have. We travel tomorrow!"

On my way to the door, I turn. "There is one other issue, my lord. I do not trust this messenger – if he is a messenger! Consider: the King has his choice of any man in Scotland, and he chooses so large a man to ride a small horse? He is a knave, I wager, but messenger he is not. If you permit me a recommendation, kill him."

The Earl frowns in frustration. "Would you have me kill the King as well?" With a nod and bow, I exit the Hall, and as always I allow the Earl the last word. I spend the night with Elizabeth.

While saying goodbye to my son, Robert, I am interrupted by the King's messenger who is eager to depart. It is November 24th, and the Earl, David, and myself keep an eye on Edward; we move quickly, traveling by horseback through the bogs and moors. We reach Edinburgh late in the afternoon; the smell of the city is evident even from far away, a putrid stench that reminds me of Woodring. We pass the loch below Edinburgh Castle; and the waters move with unnatural growths. Displayed on posts, the entrance to the city is lined with the heads of those convicted of crimes – capital offences – against the state. A hollowness fills their eyes. Their "stares" rattle my nerve, and sear themselves into my memory. We barely arrive and I already long for the return home.

At the gates of Edinburgh Castle, we are meet by Livingston, an advisor to James II, King of Scotland. He manages a fake smile. Our horses are taken to stable. We will soon be in the King's court, where, I fear thunder clouds build ominously over the throne. The storms of Scotland's newest inhumanity originate there; the worst that man can do to man, the treachery and deception with which power is so readily corrupted.

As we enter the Great Hall, the usual pleasantries are exchanged. We are then led to our assigned seats in silence. The King enters, and all bow before him. "You

St. Margaret's Chapel, Edinburgh Castle

may rise," the ten-year-old James gives his command. The Earl asks to speak; but not long into his speech about the allegiance of the Douglas clan to the throne, a decapitated bull's head is placed on the table, it's jet black color symbolic of our deaths. I hear the sound of marching soldiers; the hall fills with the King's guards. Resistance is futile. Quickly standing, we are subdued, then escorted into a courtyard lit by lamps. The young King pleads for our lives. His child's voice offers us no salvation, and I believe that he was unaware of his advisors' intentions.

The Earl will be first. William's hands and feet are bound, his eyes covered. Three guards hold his body as his neck is placed on the block. The executioner, no surprise, is Edward, our former messenger who lines up his target. With a powerful swing, life ends for the Earl. In that instant, time no longer exists. No sound touches my ears. The rain that has been falling from the sky, stops, drops of water suspended in mid-air. My heart pounds. I count each breath. Thoughts of Elizabeth and Robert race through my head. Gradually, I feel the rain falling on my face again. The soldiers holding me down. My life, or what little there is left of it, moves quickly again. I see the Earl's head roll, landing at the feet of a crying boy, who is Scotland's King. The Earl's eyes blink three last times. His body is thrown over the wall, bouncing its way down the cliff. His head is saved for display at the city gate, proof of the execution for all to view.

David is next. He puts up more a fight, but it is a resistance that cannot alter his fate. Even on the block, he continues to struggle, causing the first swing to graze his neck. He is nearly upright before a second swing removes his head, cleanly. His heart pumps on, and a fountain of blood pouring from his neck as his body falls to the ground. I am then pushed hard to the ground, my face in the dirt. With one eye, I see, sideways, the inscription above the entrance to St. Margaret's Chapel: *The souls of the righteous are in the hand of God, there shall be no evil happen to them, they are in peace.* I expect the blades swift entry into my neck; instead, I am picked up, carried below the castle, and thrown into a cell.

Locked in the darkness, I feel my way along the walls. I end up sitting in a corner, rocking back and forth, trying to keep warm. I am alone with my thoughts and wonder, *will I be forgotten, left to go mad in this dungeon?* I try to think of Elizabeth; but it is St. Margaret that dominates my thoughts, over and over: *There shall be no evil happen to them, they are in peace.*

I rest but do not sleep. Soon, I am startled by rustling in the hallway. The dim light of dawn signals the passing night. It is a new day, and I still retain the breath of life. A servant brings some water and soup, a good sign; I am to be kept alive. Three more days of this routine pass. I spend hours walking in circles, listening to rats scurry about. I name two of the gray creatures after the Kings' advisors, Livingston and Crichton. How long a day is when it is filled with nothing. I am losing my mind in the monotony of this cage.

If memory serves, it is the 28th day of November. I am weak when five men arrive carrying with them a lantern. My eyes strain while adjusting to the light. One of the men steps upon a block, hangs the lantern on a high hook. It swings, pendulum-like casting shadows one way, then the other. In anticipation, the rats begin to gather. One of the men, dressed more officially than the others announces charges of high-treason. I am shoved to the floor, and with a precise blow my head rolls off. The guards dance as drunkards, kicking the rats away from my blood. I become entertainment for the mindless and cruel, food for the rodents. My head joins the rest, lining the road into the city. My hollow stare, too pierces those that pass by and dare to look.

* * *

The seasons continue and it is now one year later. As for me, Elizabeth, I no longer exist; my execution ordered but never carried out. I live in a small cottage near the village of Kirkudbright. I rename myself "Grace", that is what Malcolm told me I possessed. From a small hill, I can still view Threave Castle, a reminder of the not so distant past, a place where ambition devours innocence, and where those who would rule are driven insane by their own vanities. Sometimes I climb the hill and have a look, but the sight turns my stomach; a man-made canyon of stone, full of mongers and minions, a building that will someday turn to rubble. I prefer the view from my cottage, the pleasant memories of my husband, and the company of our son, Robert, who bears a likeness to us both.

Shortly after the executions in Edinburgh, Woodring received orders to kill me. He escorted me to a cottage on the edge of the estate, where, because I have the appearance that men desire, he intended to ravish me first. I thought only of our son Robert, and what will become of him, as Woodring threw me near the fireplace. In an instant, I turned and ran him through with a fire-poker. I was surprised to find myself smiling faintly. Gritting my teeth, I twisted the instrument, opening up the chambers of Woodring's heart, releasing the demons living within. All the innocence remaining inside of me left as well. I buried his body deep in the garden, giving him over to the worms; the spring vegetables will serve as his only monument.

I decided to continue living in this cottage, but I spent the first few days in fear, sleeping little. One day continued into the next and no one ever inquired about Woodring. I often wonder, *what can be said about a man that no one misses*?

It seems an age since Malcolm's murder. I have pieced together the events of what has become known as *The Black Dinner*, a story of family betrayal. I now understand royal politics. Their triumphs benefit few, and their tragedies touch us all - it is a perpetual abyss. Initially, I believed that untangling the plot behind my husband's death would offer me peace; but once known only an indifference fills my thoughts about the conspiracies. I am simply left alone.

Age has taken from me all innocence and youth; my beauty is gone. I feel that one day soon "Grace" will go the way of Elizabeth. I am left to my own devices; the monotony of life consumes my days. It is November, and there is a bitterness to the cold air that fills my lungs, surrounds my soul, and causes me to shiver. The breath of life is visible upon exhale. Only in a place such as this can I feel the beating of my own heart. I have come to embrace the routine that my husband spoke of so dearly. My habits allow me a kind of security, a puny imposition of my will on nature's perpetual cycle of discord and unity.

Threave Castle

1100 An early castle is built around 1100 by Fergus, the Celtic Earl of Galloway.
1308 The earlier castle is burned by Edward Bruce (c.1280- 1318).
1300's A keep of five stories stands within a courtyard behind a wall and ditch. There are drum towers at each corner. The present castle is constructed by Archibald the Grim, 3rd Earl of Douglas (1286-1330).
Late 1300's King David II (1324-1371) chose the Black Douglas family to protect Western Scotland. Archibald the Grim became Lord of Galloway and made Threave his power base.
1440 The 6th Earl of Douglas (1424-1440) and his brother along with Sir Malcolm Fleming (d. 1440) set out from Threave for Edinburgh where they are executed at The Black Dinner.
1447 Threave is updated to withstand artillery.
1455 King James II (1430-1460) sieged Threave with artillery, the King is helped by the MacLellans. After 1455, Threave is a Royal Castle.
1513 The Maxwells are made keepers of the castle. In 1525, the Maxwell post became hereditary.
1542 After a Scottish loss to the English at the Battle of Solway Moss, the castle was given over to the English.
1545 The castle is recaptured by the Scottish Earl of Arran.
1640 The castle is besieged for thirteen weeks by an army of Covenanters until Maxwell, Earl of Nithsdale was forced to surrender. The castle's roof is removed and the structure abandoned.
1803-1815 Threave is used as a prison for French troops during the Napoleonic wars.
1948 The castle is given over to the National Trust and managed by Historic Scotland.

The Cemetery Below Edinburgh Castle

LINLITHGOW PALACE
8" x 10" oil

**Royal Residence:
Associated with Stewart (Stuart)**

Linlithgow Palace is located between the political centers of Edinburgh and Stirling. Originating in the twelfth century, the structure was the home of Scotland's monarchs. The palace was enlarged in 1301, destroyed by fire in 1350, rebuilt during the fifteenth century, and regularly expanded until 1624. It was burned in 1746 and fell into the ruin visible today. The painting captures a 2006 vantage.

The Axis

A Legend of Linlithgow Palace
(Told from the perspective of Earc Abercorn)

A messenger for Mary de Guise, I am without charge, resting. As a member of the royal court, I spend my days awaiting orders. Briskly about their errands, in contrast, are those subjects of the realm who, having come here from the far corners of the kingdom, now pass before me. Linlithgow Palace is home to our monarchs, making this courtyard the center of Scotland. A nation in miniature exists here, within these massive walls. Little more than a spectator, I watch the activity transpiring before me.

I could be summoned at any moment, but at present I pass the time sitting in front of the stone fountain commissioned by King James V. The year is 1542; the sculptors completed their work only five years ago. During the fountain's construction, I often conversed with the masons; and all those witnessing its progress were captivated by it. Passers-by marveled at the new beauty unveiled each day as the hands of man transformed the blocks. Yet now, although it is a thing of beauty, those who pass by pay it no mind. I suppose that we have both been here long enough to become common, for neither I nor the fountain garners a second glance.

From where I sit, however, this fountain is Linlithgow's jewel. A three-tiered triangle topped with a crown, the structure towers over me. Gently flowing water cascades out of the face of a sculpted sun into a circular basin, then out through the mouths of human and animal heads. It descends to an octagonal trough, decorated with a drummer and a figure bearing a scroll, and adorned with mermaids. The water pools before it can move through the mouths of angels and humans into the bottom, which is embellished with heraldic motifs. Two unicorns support the Scottish royal arms; a lion and a winged deer hold up the joined arms of Scotland and France.

Those joined "arms" belong to James V, born here at Linlithgow, and to his wife Mary de Guise, born at Bar-le-duc in Lorraine, France. In marrying French royalty, James had renewed the *Auld Alliance*, an accord sealed with a series of treaties between the two nations. His first French wife, Madeleine of Valois, died in July of 1537; the following year he wed De Guise, whose bidding I do.

James is at Falkland Palace, just to the north. He is bedridden, suffering with fever after returning from Lochmaben, where he sat out the most recent battle with the English. When Henry VIII broke from the Roman church, he asked his nephew James, my King, to do the same. James refused. Worse, he ignored a meeting with Henry at York, which prompted the English invasion. Just last month, in November, some fifteen- to eighteen-thousand Scots marched south to meet the invaders at Solway Moss. The battle ended in a crushing defeat for my King and country.

Passage Through, Linlithgow Palace

My mistress, however, is here. She is pregnant and believed to be, even now, in labor. The nation, ears turned toward this palace, awaits an heir.

Allowed no entry into the chambers and upstairs apartments, I am bored. My thoughts tumble over one another as I pace the courtyard. There's a thickening mist, but I notice the moss and grass growing in the cracks between the paving stones at my feet. Standing next to the fountain, I stick my hand in the flow, disturbing its rhythms, and take a drink. I gaze into the sky.

As the rain begins to fall, I hear the announcement echoing through the palace: Scotland has a new Queen-to-be, Mary Stewart (Stuart), born this 8th of December! The news will spread around Scotland by word of mouth; but I am sent to Falkland to inform the King directly of his daughter's arrival.

By boat, I navigate over the Firth of Forth. A short journey inland brings me to the entrance to Falkland Palace, dominated by two symmetrical stone towers. Once inside, I learn that the thirty-year old King's condition has not improved. I am quickly ushered to James' priest and give him the news regarding the birth. Through a doorway, I view the King lying motionless, laboring with each breath. His body failing, James is surrounded by physicians, nobles, and priests. On top of this, he has been spiritually ill for some time due to the loss of his two princes: James Stewart, Duke of Rothesay, born in 1540, and Robert Stewart, Duke of Albany, born in 1541, both died within a few days of one another last April. Once, when I spoke with James about their deaths, he replied, "The King has a duty to shoulder losses." However, I knew that the tragedy of losing children had taken life out of him, leaving him somber in mood and dulling his exercise of authority. I wonder what reaction the news of Mary Stewart, the couple's third child, will bring. The priest whispers in his ear; the King struggles to ask, "Is it man, or woman?"

"A daughter, Sire."

"Daughter!"

He slowly opens and closes his eyes and in a soft voice says, "The Stewarts came with a lass," (I know he means Marjorie Bruce) "and they shall pass with a lass" (he means his new daughter). Those are the last words he speaks. Following tradition, the priest instructs the King. "Give her your blessing!" The King manages a weak smile, kisses his hand, and offers it to the lords around him. With that, he turns his head away from his attendants, and all breath escapes his lungs.

On another misty day, I am there – along with the rest of the royal court – when they bury him, next to his first French wife Madeleine, at Holyrood in Edinburgh. How odd: the man, both of whose marriages were to French women, could not speak a word of the language. Yet his, in each case, was not just a union of a man and a woman, but an alliance of nations.

Nearly twenty years since, it's 1561. I remain stationed – albeit less nimbly – on a bench here in Linlithgow's courtyard. After James' death, his infant daughter Mary, then but a week old, became Queen of Scots. De Guise, my former mistress, acted as Regent for a time, from 1554 until her death of natural causes last year in Edinburgh Castle. They took her home to St. Pierre de Riems in France to lay her to rest.

My royal mistress now is that same one whose birth I announced to her father James: Mary Stewart, just back from France. They spell her name 'Stuart' there, to ensure proper pronunciation. She was only five years old when they sent her there, only

The Fountain as Centerpiece

sixteen when she married the Dauphin (who succeeded to the French throne), and only a year older than that when he died and made her a widow.

It's a dangerous and complex Scotland to which she's returned. The kingdom rises and falls daily, it seems, on marriages and murders – and now a Protestant Reformation. And this old man worries about what the future may bring, for his mistress, for all the Stewarts, and for this palace.

Linlithgow Palace

1100's The Royal Burgh is owned by King David I (c.1084-1153), and a fortification exits at the site.
1301 The castle is captured and strengthened by King Edward I (1239-1307) of England who used Linlithgow as campaign headquarters during the Wars of Independence (1295-1356).
1350 The castle is slighted until King David II (1324-1371) repairs the castle.
1424 A second house built by the Bruce Kings is destroyed by fire.
1425 Linlithgow is rebuilt by King James I (1394-1437). The property is becoming a favorite residence of the Kings of Scots.
1500's Both King James V (1512-1542) and Mary Queen of Scots (1542-1587) are born at Linlithgow. All of the Stewart kings live here prior to the Union of the Crowns in 1603.
1603 The Union of the Crowns leaves the castle under the care of a keeper.
1633 It was last used by King Charles I (1600-1649). His son James, Duke of York stayed at Linlithgow before succeeding to the throne in the Jacobite succession as James VIII (1688-1766) in 1685. (James was commonly referred to as, The Old Pretender.)
1650's Cromwell garrisons the Palace.
1680's Linlithgow Palace is visited by the future Queen Anne (1665-1714) with her father.
1745 Visiting at different times, both the commanders at the Battle of Culloden, Bonnie Prince Charlie (1720-1788) and the Duke of Cumberland (1721-1765) grace the Palace.
1746 General Hawley (1679-1759) retreats here after being defeated by the Jacobites at the nearby Battle of Falkirk. His soldiers accidentally set the Palace ablaze, and it is never restored.
2000's Linlithgow is in the care of Historic Scotland.

View from Linlithgow Palace

Linlithgow Palace, the Great Room

TRAQUAIR HOUSE
8" x 10" oil

**Family / Clan Associations:
Douglas, Maitland, Keith, Haliwick,
Craig, Lindsay, Watson, Murray, and Stewart of Buchan**

Traquair House began as a royal hunting lodge in 1107; it was enlarged in 1492 and saw regular additions through the sixteenth and seventeenth centuries. The house was later used as a refuge for Roman Catholic priests when the Stuarts of Traquair supported Mary Queen of Scots and the Jacobite cause. The painting is based on a 2008 view.

The Long Way Around

A Legend of Traquair House

Traquair lays claim to being the oldest, continuously inhabited house in Scotland. Four-hundred years ago, the River Tweed was rerouted around the structure from the end of the drive (way) for a better layout. For over 250 years, both friend and foe alike have been prohibited from using the estate's proper entrance - the Bear Gates. More monument than entry, the gates have an air of isolation about them and have remained locked for almost three-hundred years. There are no paths or tracks either on the approach to or the retreat from the gates. Well-manicured grass covers the ground, with trees lining the trail to the grand white house below. Peacocks populate the area, strutting about as if they were the royalty. The last person, in fact, to pass through the gates was Prince Charles Edward Stuart, Bonnie Prince Charlie. The 5th Earl at that time, Charles Stewart, closed the gates behind the Bonnie Prince a mere six years after their construction (the year was 1738). The Earl vowed that they would not be opened until a Stuart king was crowned in London. The Bonnie Prince, or the Young Pretender, was defeated in 1745 at the Battle of Culloden, effectively ending the Stuart's quest for the crown – and any cause to unlock those gates!

Traquair House

1100's King Alexander I (1078-1124) had a hunting lodge at Traquair.
1200's The lands are granted to the Douglases.
1200's- 1478 The lands pass through numerous families.
1300's Traquair is visited by many of the Kings of Scotland and England.
1478 The Stewart Earls of Buchan purchase the house.
1500's A new wing is added.
1513 The laird of Traquair is killed at the Battle of Flodden where England defeats Scotland.
1566 Mary, Queen of Scots (1542-1587) visits. She is accompanied by Lord Darnley (1545-1567) and their son, the future King James VI (1566-1625).
1645 The Marquis of Montrose (1612-1650), who was initially a Covenanter then a Royalist. He fled to Traquair House after the Battle of Philliphaugh where Covenanters defeat the Royalists Army. He is refused entry by the laird.
1745 Bonnie Prince Charlie (1720-1780), the Young Pretender visits the house on his way to invade England.
2000's Traquair House is privately owned.

The Bear Gates

Flags Flying over Traquair

FYVIE CASTLE
8" x 10" oil

Family / Clan Associations:
Lindsay, Preston, Meldrum, Seton, Gordon, and Forbes

Fyvie Castle began as a royal castle in the thirteenth century, the River Ythan flowed around the castle, creating a fortress of impenetrable marshes. By the late fourteenth century, ownership had passed through several families, each of whom added to the structure. A trio of additions ensued, in 1397, 1433, and 1596. The sieges of 1644 and 1650 left Fyvie, by the eighteenth century, in a damaged state; but major repairs came in 1733, followed by another expansion in 1889. Today, the castle is one of the finest in Scotland. The painting renders Fyvie's appearance in 2008.

Boundaries

A Legend of Fyvie Castle
(Told from the perspective of True Thomas)

Several years have passed since I, Thomas, received my powers of prophecy, bestowed on me by a mysterious queen. But it seems as if I am only now meeting her, during a hunt near the lands of my village, on the estate of Melrose Abbey. I fall asleep under the Eildon tree and am lost from this world's sight in a seven-year fantasy. It is the Queen of the Elves herself who seduces me, her kiss that carries me away. Her face like that of an angel, the rest of her cloaked in softest green silk and velvet, she seems utterly unsubstantial. I am instantly caught in her spell and go with her. We ride a gray steed that gallops like the wind. He carries us – and the fifty-nine silver bells that hang from his mane, one for each elf in her kingdom – into the hills.

I enter this strange realm and am welcomed by creatures, half-animal and half-human. Elves, small in stature but large in heart, are introduced. I am shown a garden and given an apple. "Take this for thy wages, Thomas," the Queen commands; "it will give thee a tongue that can never lie." I eat. I cease to be *Thomas the Rymer*, as I had been known; now I am *True Thomas*. The Queen then explains that I may never speak of what I see or hear in Elfland, on penalty of being prohibited ever to return.

While I live with the elves, I never sleep. But, eventually tiring, I am lost in a dream of returning home. I awake alone, beneath the tree, in the very spot from which I had departed this world.

The passing of time inevitably changes heart and home, but I look at my hands and realize that they have not aged. And I arrive home to all things as they were. I soon learn that my seven years in Elfland have been but a week of life in my village. Still, my family and friends look at me like a ghost.

I am different thereafter, taller, more confident. I see the world differently, too: not in a passing moment, but in a strangely wider view, encompassing the ever-changing seasons and extending into eternity. On occasion, I can move the veil of time, a curtain of silk with a velvet rope that opens to the future. I pull it back to predict the death of our King, Alexander III. I also foretell other events from visions received. Often I am perplexed, wondering, *how does one describe events that have not occurred, but will?* I deliver other prophecies – of the Battle of Bannockburn, of the Jacobite uprisings, of the Union of the Crowns that join Scotland and England. With a tongue of truth, I journey around the nation. So often surrounded by those wanting what I know, I periodically seek the refuge and solitude of the trees.

***

Years later, I am invited north, by the Abbot of a Cistercian priory, to mediate a land dispute. The monks' properties border the Fyvie Estate. I do not realize that, before the trip ends, I will pronounce a curse!

It's to boundary stones that land claims typically appeal; and those marking the end of Fyvie and the beginning of the Priory have been removed. The Abbot is worried; he suspects an attempt to seize their lands. I go, unannounced, to the wooden castle. I am about to enter the unmanned gates, when a fast-moving storm, driven by the wind, suddenly slams them shut. I regard this as an omen of doom. The wind ceases while I'm standing before the closed gates, but neither man nor nature re-opens them. After a moment's wait, I make my way back to the Abbey.

I tell the monks the story; they inform me that the gates have stood open continuously for seven years. As the conversation unfolds, my suspicions that Fyvie's masters have shut me out harden. Resenting their unwillingness to receive me, I proclaim the following curse on the castle: "So long as the three boundary stones remain missing and displaced, the laird's eldest son will never inherit the Fyvie Estate." I also share with the monks what I foresee: that the simple structure will eventually be transformed into a great stone building, among the finest in the nation.

I leave the next morning, heading south. After two days of travel, I arrive at the village outskirts and stop at the Eildon tree, where I first encountered the Queen of the Elves. In time, she appears, her beauty moving me as on the first day I met her. I ask her what she knows about the matter of the boundary stones. "Your curse is valid and can only be broken if the stones are returned to their original locations," she replies. "However," she goes on, "this is unlikely: the first stone is being used in the building of a new tower; the second stone will be thrown into the River Ythen and thus will never be found; the third is on display in the castle, kept in a basin on account of the water – the tears of the disinherited! – constantly seeping from it. Unlike most estates, which remain in their families through inheritance, Fyvie will pass from one family to the next."

Her words fade, and I feel as old as the tree. I have grown weary of the future, stretching out endlessly before me; my joy comes increasingly from past memories. It is 1297, and I look up at the sky from beneath a sanctuary of branches. The Queen has vanished, but left me her cloak. I pull it over me and am draped with the sweet peace of what has been. All Scotland looks down on me from above; I hear them calling my name.

Fyvie Castle

1214 King William the Lyon (c.1142-1214) holds court at Fyvie Castle, as does King Alexander II (1198-1249) in 1222.
1296 King Edward I of England (1239-1307) stays at Fyvie during the Wars of Independence.
1308 King Robert the Bruce (1274-1329) stays here.
1380 Fyvie passed from the Crown to the Lindsay family.
1402 The property passes to the Prestons. In 1433, the estate belongs to the Meldrums.
1596 The property is owned by the Seton Earls of Dunfermline.
1620 The largest pearl in the crown of Scotland is found in the River Ythan and placed in the royal crown.
1644 The Marquis of Montrose (1612-1650) occupies the castle.
1650 The castle is held by Cromwellian forces.
1689-90 The Setons are Jacobites and fortify the castle following the Rising.
1733 Fyvie passes to the Gordon, Earls of Aberdeen.
1889 Alexander Forbes-Leith (1847-1925), steel magnate, buys Fyvie for £175,000.
By 1900's Five families including: Prestons – Meldrum – Setons – Gordons- Forbes Leith, each added towers creating the current castle.
1982 The castle is managed by the National Trust for Scotland.

Imposing Entrance - Fyvie

SCOTLAND: CASTLES & CLANS THE LEGENDS

NEIDPATH CASTLE
36" x 12" oil

**Family / Clan Associations:
Fraser, Hay, Douglas, and Wemyss**

Neidpath Castle stands on a steep bank above the River Tweed. The castle dates from around 1200, with the construction of a keep and other additions coming in the fourteenth century. The structure was expanded and fortified further in the sixteenth and seventeenth centuries. The siege of 1650 left Neidpath in ruins, the subsequent partial restoration of which is still visible today, alongside the unrestored sections. In an 1803 poem, William Wordsworth lamented the cutting down of Neidpath's woods; but the area is forested today. The painting is from a visit in 2008.

Side by Side

A Legend of Neidpath Castle
(Told from the perspective of Bernard of Kilwinning)

The year is 1306. I prefer the lands of my home and count my steps when traveling on foreign soil. Time, for me, moves more slowly as I walk upon unfamiliar earth. I am most at peace at Arbroath Abbey, where I am serving as the Abbot. In Scotland, my fellow countrymen call me Bernard. After an arduous journey, I arrive in London to verify the deaths of William Wallace and Simon Fraser – Scotland's freedom fighters.

The city surrounds me; boats pass by on the River Thames. The continual bustle of folk moving to and fro unnerves me. The path to the Tower of London lies along a cobblestone street. Near the end, I see two boys viewing the impaled heads that are on display, both as proof of death and as warning to others. The dead never blink, but the children are having a contest to see if one of them will. They stand, shoulder to shoulder, one looking into the skull of William Wallace, his friend peering into Simor Fraser's bulging eyes. The boys remain still for a long time, but finally can't resist a peek at one another. The taller one gives the other a push.

When they start to mimic the dead men's expressions, I intervene. They run circles around me until I gather them up and sit them down with force. I instruct them not to speak, stare, or copy any of my mannerisms; and then I begin to tell them the story of the two men, Wallace and Fraser, to whom the skulls belong.

The boys settle down as I begin, "Those men once represented the independence of Scotland. I know it does not appear so - the current display lacking all nobility and respect - but life is not always what it seems, and the dead have stories to tell. Fraser and Wallace were defiant to the end; and when they met their deaths in this city, both were, as you know, hung, drawn and quartered. The heads are here, but their other appendages were sent to the far reaches of England."

Before continuing, I shift my weight and move my cane to the other side. The boys look up in anticipation; more comfortable, I begin, "These men bravely defied your country's rule, because the people to the far north are, by nature, uncompromising. And the spirit of freedom that lived within them, now indwells the entire Kingdom of Scotland."

My cane touches the tops of their heads, punctuating what I say. "Now, before you boys get up, I want you to give this old abbot some respect. "Do I have your attention?" Wide-eyed, they do not speak but quickly shake their heads in agreement.

"The Lowlands," I emphasize, " are where two kingdoms meet. It is a region of turbulence because they are a natural corridor for invasion. So, look" – I point my cane at the two vanquished Scots – "but do not stare at their heads, boys!" And I begin to teach.

Wallace was born in Airdrie and Fraser in Peebleshire. And as you boys are side by side, so once were they, fight-

Neidpath, the Approach

ing the invading forces of England in the war for Scottish Independence. When their legs were attached to their bodies, they walked this earth. Those eyes once looked on the ones they loved; those mouths drew the breath of life; those ears once heard the sounds of nature; those lips uttered words of inspiration. The patriots that are now before us in death, once stood next to one another in the struggle for freedom.

I pause again before the smaller boy commands me, "Continue on!"

When Wallace was fifteen, not much older than you lads, he was in the care of the church at Dundee until the age of seventeen. William was the middle brother, the oldest was Malcolm and the youngest was John. Following tradition, the eldest inherited the lands and titles, the younger brothers were educated by the church.

When Longshanks – or Edward I, the English King – exiled King John Balliol, and tried to restore a Guardian of Scotland to the government, he required the Scots first to pay him homage. William's father Sir Malcolm Wallace, a knight, would not take the oath, and leaving his wife Margaret and their younger sons in the care of her father Sir Ranald Cranford, he and his son Malcolm took refuge in the north. William went to live with his uncle and soon displayed the skill and courage that made him a leader. He towered, too, above his countrymen, standing six foot seven inches.

Wallace's friend, Sir Simon Fraser of Peebleshire, obtained notoriety by stealing Edward's horses during a siege at Caerlaverock Castle in 1300. A knight, he fought alongside Andrew Murray, Wallace's co-commander at the victorious Battle of Stirling Bridge. Murray was mortally wounded in the battle, considered the first in the Wars of Scottish Independence. Fraser then led the Scots to victory at the Battle of Roslin, fighting alongside John Comyn III, Lord of Badenoch - also known as the Red Comyn. After the battle in Roslin, King Edward I marched north, through Sterling, to take Perth, then headed south to Dunfermline. The Bishops of St. Andrews and Glasgow with the Red Comyn met Edward's army and swore fealty. Fraser refused, and did not even attend the meeting.

At this point, the children were losing interest; but I continued speaking to the small crowd that gathered:

The resistance continued to 1304, and Fraser fought with William Wallace at the Battle of Happrew, where they suffered defeat. Fraser later fought for King Robert I of Scotland (Robert the Bruce). He escaped after Bruce's defeat at the Battle of Methven, but was captured in 1306. Fraser was sent to London and executed. Wallace was soon captured, too, and joined Fraser in death.

Once again, a tap of my cane captures the children's attention, and I speak to them in a whisper. "Remember lads: freedom lives in the heart, then travels to the mind, and expresses itself in actions. Now be off with you, and know that the Kingdom of England shall not reign over

Neidpath Castle, from the River Tweed

Scotland." Counting my steps back to my homeland, I return to Arbroath Abbey having seen with my own eyes the heads of our patriots.

* * *

Many years have passed since I viewed Wallace and Fraser. In 1320, I drafted the Declaration of Arbroath, a letter addressed to Pope John XXII that asked him to overturn the 1305 Papal recognition of England's supremacy over Scotland. I remembered my time in London when I dipped quill into ink ending the declaration with these words: *for, as long as but a hundred of us remain alive, never will we on any conditions be brought under English rule. It is in truth not for glory, nor riches, nor honours that we are fighting, but for freedom – for that alone, which no honest man gives up but with life itself.* Before being sent to Rome, the document was signed by fifty-one magnates and nobles of Scotland. My words were written in behalf of Robert the Bruce in an effort to secure recognition for him as the legitimate King of Scotland. They also called on the Pope to remove the excommunication of Robert for the murder of the Red Comyn (John Comyn II) at Dumfries Church in 1306.

I was grateful when the Pope accepted the Scottish cause –even if the English did not! And I'm grateful to have lived to see – with the Treaty of Edinburgh-Northampton three years ago, in 1328 – the end of the great war for independence that began in the year of my birth, 1296, with the English invasion. But, near death now – this year of our Lord, 1331 – I can only wonder how many more wars must be fought before the freedom for my country, for which Wallace and Fraser died, becomes a reality.

Neidpath Castle

1300 Sir Simon Fraser (d.1307) owns the keep. He is known for stealing Edward's I (1239-1307) horses and armor at the siege of Caerlaverock Castle.
1303 Sir Simon Fraser defeats the English at the Battle of Roslin.
1307 Sir Simon Fraser is executed in London, England.
1312 Neidpath passes to the Hays of Yester by the marriage of Sir Simons daughter, Mary (the heiress). She married Sir Gilbert de Haya of Yester.
1500's Neidpath is substantially remodeled.
1563 Mary Queen of Scots (1542-1587) stays at the castle, as does her son King James VI (1566-1625) in 1587.
1650 The castle held out against Cromwell's army longer than any other stronghold in southern Scotland.
1686 Douglas, Duke of Queensberry purchases the castle.
1803 Sir Walter Scott (1771-1832) and William Wordsworth (1770-1850) both visit the castle.
1810 Neidpath passes to the Earl of Wemyss and March.
2000's Neidpath Castle remains under the Earl of Wemyss ownership.

Arched Gate

DUNURE CASTLE
10" x 20" oil

**Family / Clan Associations:
Kennedy**

Dunure Castle originated as a keep in the thirteenth century, which was expanded and fortified in the fifteenth and sixteenth centuries. By 1696 it was in ruin. The castle was the ancestral home of the Kennedy's of Carrick, who ruled over much of southwestern Scotland. The painting draws on a 2008 view.

Webs of Betrayal

A Legend of Dunure Castle

Alone, night after night, Lord Dunure, the 4th Earl of Cassilis, can be found in the Great Hall of his castle. The lord is a portly fellow, with eyes bloodshot from lack of sleep. Bored with his daily existence and lacking suitable company, he sometimes simply paces back and forth, stopping occasionally to warm his hands at the fireplace. More often, he kneels for hours in a candle-lit corner of the room – for so long, in fact, that he rises with difficulty. Many might think, more might hope, that he is praying. Instead, he is studying some small creatures of his kingdom – spiders!

The Hall, dark and cold, mirrors his own heart; the castle servants try to steer clear of both. Most people, in fact, go to great lengths to avoid this lord, otherwise known as Gilbert Kennedy. Critical and manipulative, subject to fits of rage, he is the worst of company. Any charm his character once possessed has long since been displaced by madness.

Remaining Ruins and Dovecot

Gilbert is obsessed with the spiders' fierce determination to invade the space of his Hall. Their webs traverse every crack, crevice, and corner; they bridge every tiny chasm. At times, Gilbert removes all the webs, only to have them reappear the next night. Other times, on his knees, he often pokes the webs to watch the spiders rush to the scene, and then squishes them between his thumb and forefinger, a coy smile pasted on his face. He admires these creatures; however, this admiration puts no restraint on his desires. Taking delight in holding the creatures' lives in his hands, Gilbert often observes them before delivering death. How precisely, deliberately, effortlessly these small arachnids go about their work! Gilbert resolves to mimic their methods. He will apply their designs to his ambitions.

The late 1500's are a time of turmoil in Scotland. A great land transfer is underway, an unintended effect of the Protestant Reformation. Gilbert himself becomes a Protestant by marriage. He is eager to cash in, and during the long nights watching the spiders, this lord conceives his plan. To fulfill his insatiable greed, Gilbert will spin webs of his own. Thinking of nothing else, he lets his own passions consume him. He looks not to the immortality of the afterlife, but to the material possessions that entrap a mortal soul.

The clock is ticking as Catholic holdings throughout Scotland are being transferred. The time for action is drawing near, and Gilbert hears rumors about a monk at Glenluce Abby. The weakness of this man's character prior to his conversion tempts Gilbert to ask himself, *could he once again be persuaded to corruption?* The web Gilbert spins is not large: a small bribe yields all the necessary forged signatures, permitting most of the Abbey lands to pass to the Earl. A sense of accomplishment fills Gilbert's being. He sits drinking in the Great Hall, watching his spiders and celebrating their powers of entanglement. He talks to them, and his voice echoes throughout the Hall, as if to inform the uninvited that their designs are not as grand as his. But there is no response; only silence returns to Gilbert. It is in this isolation that a small part of him grows anxious with worry. Questions about the monk's loyalty race through his mind. He paces, wondering if the character flaws he has exploited could be exploited by others, possibly to his own destruction. *I have the Abbey lands,* Gilbert thinks, *but at the price of this monk's weakness.* And he takes the intrigue to fresh depths with a fatal decision: *This monk is not the Pope's, he's mine; and if he's mine, I can do with him as I wish.* As the spiders spin larger webs, so would Gilbert. A web grand enough to entangle the monk is required.

The Earl knows of an assassin; and they quickly agree on a sum. Gilbert impatiently awaits news of the monk's demise; it comes by messenger. Payment is transferred, and again, the Earl is smug with achievement. If only for a moment, happiness fills his hollow existence. But as the spiders always return, so does the worry that haunts his soul. This night, the creatures infuriate him. He is jealous of the ease of their existence, the effortlessness with which they spin webs and trap their prey. Day after day they repeat their work; Gilbert is addicted to watching them. Sitting near the fireplace, he thinks about past events and tries to imagine how the future will unfold. His thoughts end in confusion as the spiders once again capture his attention. He envies the simplicity of their lives, the sameness of their days; the spiders face none of the messy aftermath that plague human plots.

Exhausted, Gilbert falls asleep in his chair and dreams about becoming tangled in his own web. He awakes with fear, not of losing what he has, but of losing who he is. He looks through a web into one of the chasms. In the darkness, he sees demons, his own face among them. In a frightening moment of moral reflection, Gilbert realizes that he is not like the spiders; he is far above them! Driven deeper in madness, he orders the servants to rid the entire castle of all the diminutive creatures.

Gilbert's mind rushes on. If he cannot trust a monk, then how can his faith in an assassin hold? The Earl's doubts continue to grow, charges are trumped up, and not unlike the vanquished caught in the spider's web, the assassin dangles from the galley. The Earl sits with his spiders, pleased with the outcome. In silence, he puts his hand over his heart and gazes heavenward. Though only an Earl, he feels like a king! He is the master of the webs, being the only one left alive who knows the truth. And what kind man would betray himself?

For a time, life at the castle continues without incident. The Earl gives little thought to the two lives he has taken. On occasion their voices echo around the chambers of his vacant heart, but his own pursuits trump any remorse. As part of his daily routine, he proudly rides his horse to the edges of the estate. During one of his trips, he becomes more conscious of his beating heart believing it an omen of impending doom.

That night, the Earl awakens to find a spider crawling on his arm. He stares at its little body. He brings his thumb and forefinger up to crush it, but stops, studies the tiny creature and then returns it to the floor. This night he is not in the Hall but in his bedroom. Now

Along the Coast, Firth of Clyde

fully awake, his obsession overtakes him: he will spin an even greater web, this time at the Abbey of Crosseguel.

Things begin poorly when the Earl approaches the monks with bribery and finds none who will accept. The Abbot, Quinton Kennedy, Gilbert's uncle, had warned the monks of the Earl's unscrupulousness, long before his overture. Still, when Quentin suddenly dies, and is replaced by a commandator (administrator) named Alan Stewart, the Earl sees a window of opportunity. And, after five years' worth of ploys fail, he has Alan kidnapped, carried to the castle, and imprisoned. Alan persists in defiance until he is led deep within the kitchens of Dunure, tied to a spit, and roasted over an open fire, one turn, then two, and Stewart signs over the Abbey.

Alan survives, and later takes his case before royalty. The webs of Gilbert's spinning, as in his dream, are finally being spun around him. Before he dies after falling from his horse, the Earl is ordered by the Scottish authorities to pay lifelong restitution to Alan. In the end, Gilbert himself is given over to the spiders, those methodical spinners of webs, consumers of the hapless victims that fall into them. After his death, his wife Margaret Lyon, carries on with their two sons. It is rumored that she spends her days clearing the castle of webs.

Dunure Castle

1200's A keep existed. One tradition states that the castle was built by the MacKinnons. They were granted the estate by King Alexander III (1241-1286) as a reward for their contributions to the Scottish victory at the Battle of Largs in 1263.
1357 The Kennedys of Carrick are granted the lands.
From the 1300's The property belongs to the Kennedys of Dunure.
1400's A block of buildings is added.
1429 There is a meeting at Dunure between James Campbell who represents King James I (1394-1437) of Scotland and John Mar MacDonald representing the Lord of the Isles. MacDonald is killed, James moves to stem the outrage by executing Campbell. This "gesture" does not prevent the uprising against the King.
1570 Allan Stewart, Commendator of Crossraguael Abbey is tortured at Dunure Castle by Gilbert Kenndy, 4th Earl of Cassillis.
1573 Mary Queen of Scots (1542-1587) stays at the castle on her Royal tour down the West Coast to Glenluce Abbey then onto Whithorn Priory. At Dunure, she is the guest of Gilbert Kennedy, the 4th Earl of Cassillis (c. 1541-1576).
1650's Dunure is destroyed by an explosion, and by 1696 the castle was abandoned and ruined.
2000's The castle is privately owned.

View to Alisa Craig

Over the Horizon

HUME CASTLE
8" x 10" oil

Family / Clan Associations:
Hume

Hume Castle stands on a hill with views in every direction. A structure has existed at this location from the thirteenth century. The formidable castle was destroyed in 1515 and rebuilt four years later, only to be besieged in 1547 and 1569, and destroyed again in 1650. The current "castle" is a folly, built in 1794 on the foundations of the original structure. The painting renders a 2004 view.

Larger Schemes

A Legend of Hume Castle
(Told from the perspective of Coll Eaton)

My home, Hume Castle, stands like a beacon near the border of Scotland and England. A stonemason by trade and a soldier by necessity, I have had, all my life, a double interest in her walls. Even now, I spend my time fortifying the very bulwarks whose protection I enjoy. Through the years, the masonry has consumed most of my days, but not without frequent interruption. Clan raids occur with frequency here in the Lowlands; and as the skirmishes come and go, I periodically trade my trowel for a sword.

Wars are another matter. They change the fundamentals of society dramatically, including the leadership hierarchy – as we learned so well in 1513. Everyone here then reported to the Steward, who answered to Alexander, 3rd Lord of Hume, who himself was subject to our monarch, King James IV. The day of the Battle of Flodden, the day that within a week came to be known as *Black Friday*, was pure chaos. But who knew that the Kingdom of Scotland would be leaderless in its wake?

Scotland's finest repopulated the county of Northumbria, England, that day, as we followed our King,

Current Castle Residents

James IV, into battle. He had declared war on England to honor the *Auld Alliance*, a series of treaties dating back to 1295, which united us with France against England. We Scottish invaders, 29,000 strong, were led by the Hume, Huntly, Errol, Crawford, Montrose, Lennox, and Argyll families. Some 23,000 Englishmen faced us, led by the Lord Admiral and the forces of Surrey, Edmund, and Howard, with Dacre's Cavalry backing them up.

I was attached to the forces of Hume and Huntly, assembled on Flodden Hill; we were the vanguard, standing eight-thousand strong. Opposite us, on Branxton Hill, were Edmund's and Howard's men, against whom we had early success, until Dacre's Cavalry routed us all.

The marsh in the middle of the valley was soon stained with Scottish blood. There were many dead on Pipers Hill, on the English side; but most lay in the marshy ground below. Some Scottish horsemen appeared briefly on Branxton Hill, but they were quickly driven off by the English. On the opposing hill, Surrey's men took possession of Borthwick's silent Scottish guns. I set out across the countryside, back to my Scottish home, never setting foot on English soil since.

A year later, I spoke to a clerk from the writing office in Edinburgh. Charged with documenting the battle, he visited Hume Castle and questioned a few of us who had survived. I daresay that I learned more from him than he from me, about what he described as the largest battle, to date, between the two kingdoms. I already knew, of course, that Flodden ended in a crushing defeat for us; but the details, some of which I also knew, were staggering. Every noble family of Scotland lost a member. King James IV was killed, along with his son Alexander. They were joined in death by nine earls, fourteen Lords of Parliament, and several Highland chiefs. The Archbishop of St. Andrews had also been killed, along with other prominent churchmen. The English took few prisoners and suffered casualties amounting to 1,500. In contrast, some 10,000 Scots were lost, approximately a third of our army.

The clerk returned before long to Edinburgh, and I to my work. Here, there is always stone to lift and place, when there's not a raid to repel. This is my home.

Hume Castle

1200's The lands are held by the Homes who build the first castle.
1473 The Homes are made Lords.
1513 Alexander, 3rd Lord Home (d. 1516), led the vanguard at the Battle of Flodden. He is one of the few nobles that escaped the battle.
1516 The Regent Albany seizes Hume Castle, ravages the lands and executes the 3rd Lord Home, Alexander and his brother for treason.
1547 George, the 4th Lord, was killed before the Battle of Pinkie. After the defeat of the Scots, the English occupied the Home's lands.
1568 The Homes fight against Mary Queen of Scots (1542-1587) at the Battle of Langside where the Regent Moray defeats Mary.
1575 Alexander Home, 5th Lord of Home dies in captivity after he was arrested and convicted of treason by King James VI (1566-1625).
1605 Alexander, 6th Lord of Home (c. 1566-1619) was a favorite of King James VI (1566-1625). He was made Earl of Home.
1650 The castle is surrendered to Colonel Fenwick, one of Cromwell's commanders.
1700's The property passes to the Home Earls of Marchmont.
1794 The castle being almost level to the ground is rebuilt as a crude folly that incorporates the foundations of the original castle.
2000's Hume Castle is managed by the Clan Home Association under the guidance of Historic Scotland.

Below the Castle

Countryside - Hume

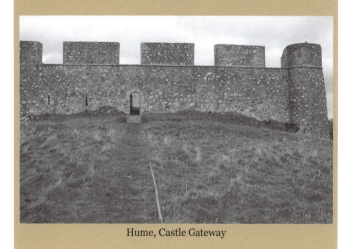

Hume, Castle Gateway

ABERDOUR CASTLE
8" x 10" oil

**Family / Clan Associations:
Mortimer, Douglas, and Watson**

Located in the center of Aberdour village, the castle dates to the eleventh century. The structure gained a keep in 1240, roughly the same time that a high stone wall replaced the mote. The sixteenth and seventeenth centuries brought expansion; but a fire in 1715 left the castle largely in ruins by 1725, upon which final destruction fell in 1844. The painting depicts Aberdour as seen in 2008.

Beneath the Surface

A Legend of Aberdour Castle

No respecter of persons, nature treats royalty and commoner alike. The Firth of Forth waters are a particularly treacherous stretch; boats are tossed to and fro before disappearing altogether into the sea. The year is 1123, and King Alexander I is traveling with his entourage from Stirling to Edinburgh. The turbulence created by a fast moving storm overtakes the King's ship. Finding themselves suddenly overboard, frantic efforts grant little relief. On the surface, waves crash; but here below, all sounds are muffled. Lungs, a moment before filled with air, are now heavy with water. It's a quick burial, but lacking any ritual. One by one, the bodies descend from light into darkness.

Chosen by God yet rejected by the sea, one lone royal survivor washes up on the shores of Inchcolm Island. His body lies at the feet of a holy man, who stands in the eye of storms. The King receives sanctuary with a monk skilled at bringing order from chaos; he nurses Alexander back to health. After his recovery, the King founds an Abbey on the island, dedicated to Scotland's famous saint, Columba.

* * *

The Firth's storms rage on, and over one-hundred years later, William de Mortimer is sent by his wife to look for their son, Jonathan. An aloof child who speaks little, he - it is rumored - has heightened senses, and can tell when the days of mortals are coming to an end. This ability troubles his father; little children should not know so much of life and death. The boy often points at people saying, "The rising is coming, which is different from the descending." Such prophecies of death make other people nervous and create awkward social encounters; these keep the child in isolation.

William searches the village, looking first where the other children play. He hopes, if only once, to find his son befriending others. Walking down to the shore, he locates Jonathan throwing rocks into the Firth, skipping them across the surface. The rocks stay afloat for but a moment, and then the sea swallows them. Jonathan turns, looks at his father holds his finger to his lips, and shakes his head, "Dah, listen to the sound of the rock falling into the depths." In a whisper, "Listen, in a second it will hit the bottom."

Confused and concerned, William scolds his son. Jonathan kneels down and begins stacking rocks into a column.

Ruins of Aberdour Castle

William snatches him away, declaring, "Whatever the sea takes, it does not give back."

William returns the next day from his nearby home at Aberdour Castle. Launching his boat, he inadvertently knocks over the cairn his son had previously built. Mumbling, William begins to board, but then stops, steps back, and re-stacks the stone column before climbing into the boat. It is a rare day of sun, and sweat pours down William's face as he rows over a murky stretch of still water. His destination is the abbey located on Inchcolm Island.

The journey is to a meeting, the agenda of which concerns an appointment by the Abbot. An argument arises over the installation of a man some view as wicked. William wants the appointment, the Abbot does not; the monks support their leader. The meeting abruptly adjourns, Mortimer exits the abbey for the return trip. Across the water, he docks his boat on the mainland and looks over to the Inchcolm with disdain.

The clouds move in quickly; and a driving rainstorm covers the earth. At times, the drops seem to come sideways, with force. Mortimer finds refuge under a tree next to his son's cairn. The clouds pass; soon long shadows return. The rhythmic rocking of his boat, mirrored upside down on the shimmering water is the last view William ever sees. Under a large branch, he dies peacefully. But despite William's wish to be buried on Inchcolm Island, and regardless of his leaving land to the Abbey, the Abbot soon reveals that he does not want the Baron's body. He believes that the family is cursed as evidenced by the child's prophetic powers.

After William's funeral on the mainland, they load his body on the boat. The Abbot, watching from the opposing shore, calls on God for help. A strong wind comes up, and the remains of Mortimer fall overboard into stormy waters. His body, wrapped and prepared for burial, disappears; he sinks quickly into the abyss, descending through the depths, disturbing the calm below. In a cold darkness, unable to overcome the weight of water, William haunts the deep. Sailors say his ghost wanders aimlessly beneath the surface in the waters that bear his name, *Mortimer's Deep*.

Aberdour Castle

1240 A high stone keep is constructed around a wooden motte.
1325 The estate, including castle, is given to Thomas Randolph, Earl of Moray (d. 1332) after he played a key part in war for Scottish Independence. Randolph is a friend and captain for Robert the Bruce (1274-1329).
1342 The property belongs to the Douglases.
1456 The Douglases are made Earls of Morton.
1500's James Douglas held the highest offices of state under Queen Mary (1542-1587) serving as her Lord High Chancellor, then Regent of Scotland during her imprisonment in England.
1581 James Douglas is beheaded by King James VI (1566-1625) who was Mary's son. Douglas is executed for unsolved crimes surrounding the death of Lord Darnley (1542-1567) – Mary's second husband and James VI's father.
1630 The castle is extended.
1688 and **1715** Parts of the castle burn.
1725 The castle is abandoned, and the family moves to the nearby Aberdour House - formally known as Cuttlehill.
Until 1791 One wing of the castle is occupied by Robert Watson of Muirhouse.
1814 Much of the keep collapses, followed by further destruction in 1919.
1924 The castle is put in the care of the state and managed by Historic Scotland.

Over the Bridge, Aberdour Castle

HERMITAGE CASTLE
9" x 16" oil

Family / Clan Associations:
Dacre, DeSoulis, Graham, Douglas, Hepburn, Stewart, and Scott

---

Hermitage Castle is described as the Guardhouse of the bloodiest valley in Britain. Located on the border of Scotland and England, Hermitage is named after a holy man who lived by the nearby Liddel Water. The stonework began during the thirteenth century with a keep added in the fourteenth century. Hermitage was besieged in 1320, restored by 1390, and further fortified in the fifteenth century. Having fallen into ruin by the early 1700's, the castle underwent partial restoration later that century. The painting is based on a 2006 view.

Prophecies

A Legend of Hermitage Castle
(Told from the perspective of Torradan Crosar)

As an armorer in the blacksmith shop, I am normally among my brethren at ground level. To escape the heat, I occasionally move to higher, better ventilated chambers; in this lofty isolation my thoughts are clear. The window reveals the world from the caphouse of Hermitage Castle, a fortress with towering walls, and my home. From here, the village unfolds before me; smoke pours from a hundred chimneys. When I tire of that view, my attention shifts to horizons that span the hills reaching towards the sea.

The sun is dipping below the horizon and the shadows are lengthening; but neither invokes the the isolation and loneliness that once defined the fortress. These were the characteristics of the man who built it, our former laird, William de Soulis. He was large, imposing, and many believed unmovable. He walked hunched over - from the weight of his own sin, if you ask me. I shudder to think of his dabbling in witchcraft and child abduction; then I smile to remember the children, however fearful, mimicking him, by bending at the waist and making funny faces to entertain the onlookers.

From this very window, I often caught sight of William, going or coming from the castle; the vison always left me cold. There was such an emptiness about him; I believe he took delight in the suffering of others. Walking next to him, more often than not, was his tall Wizard, who had once prophesied William's indestructibilty, declaring that the laird counld not be harmed by a metal weapon and could only be bound by a rope made of sand. There was no conversation with William that did not have his alleged immortality as its first topic.

I am pulled from my memories as a sudden breeze moves across my face; I catch the sound of the Liddel River. This stretch of it, as wide as two men are tall, and fed from the surrounding moorland, is a refuge for birds. I turn slightly to see Donnan Graham, catching fish – no doubt, skillfully - from his favorite spot, a large rock upon the bank. Donnan and his two younger brothers work with me in the blacksmith's shop. They are good lads, even if sometimes devious. As with most young men, they are constantly in need of instruction and discipline. However, as the recent events flood my memory again, I celebrate that rebellious streak in them that led Hermitage out of the bondage William imposed. Our saviors arrived in the form of those three unruly boys.

From beginning to end, their plan took only one month to complete. It started with Donnan passing time on the banks of the river, staying even through the frequent and fast moving storms. The wind and rain sometimes knocked down abandoned bird nests, which Donnan would pick up and observe. One might have thought he was searching for eggs; but he was holding the nests carefully to study how the twigs were woven together. He needed one of Nature's perfect designs in order to satisfy the demands of the prophecy. Seeing something useful, Donnan discarded the nest, grabbed a handful of sand from the bank, and smiled as it slipped between his fingers and fell into the water below.

With a lightness in his step, Donnan walked back to the castle. But, as he entered the courtyard, he encountered William, his arms raised and looking into the sky, declaring his dominion over his lands and announcing his control over the seasons. The courtyard was full of puddles from a recent rain, and seeing himself reflected upside down in the water, William stomped into it, sending the water splashing over the nearest bystander – Donnan. Was he imagining his influence, represented by his likeness in the water, being extended in the act?

To avoid such abuse, the elders in the community always simply moved the other way upon sight of the laird. Most of the youth were less subtle; they'd run past him, William grunting and grasping at them. Donnan, however, a rather portly child and so not as fleet of foot as the other children at Hermitage, often got splashed. Yet he typically stood, defiantly taking the baths – as again on this day.

Many underestimated Donnan, accordingly. Yet he and his two brothers were unusually brave; even if there was no appearance of them being up to something, I knew better. There were ways to create just about anything in the blacksmith's shop, and no one should have been surprised at the Grahams' willingness to apply their skill to a plot against William.

Besides this, the Grahams frequently gave as good as they got, their antics often overlooked by the villagers because they were directed at William, whom everyone loathed. Donnan's methods typically involved small distractions that concealed larger ambitions. He would gather a group of children, give one a long stick, instructing him to run at William and poke him; the laird would quickly scurry back to his chambers and the company of his Wizard. Then the real plot would unfold!

The brothers, orphans, looked after one another; and although Donnan, Rory, and Tavish had their childish moments, when they worked together, the three were unstoppable. But I always kept my eye on Donnan, as did William. Even when, at a young age, the boys emerged as a threat, William's intuition told him that Donnan was responsible for the other children's rebellion. So to insure that the subjects of William De Soulis remained under his rule, and to quash the rebellion, he consulted his Wizard. The Wizard's solution: to conjure up a Robin Redcap who could rid Hermitage of the Grahams.

Meanwhile, Rory, the middle brother, was hiding in Hermitage's Great Hall and moving the laird's possessions around, randomly. The Wizard blamed this annoyance on supernatural beings, usually ghosts. Listening to his explanations, the brothers would shake their heads in agreement; and the more the Wizard rambled on about the hauntings, the more the children would encourage him, pretending to believe him.

In any event, Rory was well-positioned to overhear the Wizard describing a Redcap to William:

This creature is a kind of goblin, native to the Lowlands of Scotland; they are rare but not impossible to find. Once one is summoned, he roams the area, killing in order to keep fresh the bloodstains on his hat: if the stains dry, then the Redcap dies. The creatures are very quick, despite their metal-bound boots and heavy pick. They only way to escape one is to quote a passage from the Holy Bible, whereupon it loses one of its teeth and becomes distracted. Nevertheless, I must warn that the Redcap is to be feared, and that, once summoned, to be rid of him is virtually impossible.

Without hesitation, William commanded the Wizard, "Summon the Redcap and have it kill the Graham brothers. After the goblin has completed its mission, we will remove its cap thus leading to its death." While William was filled with anticipation, Rory made off with his new knowledge, along with some bread from the laird's kitchen. The boy was excited to tell his older brother about the new creature they would have to torment; and upon hearing the news, Donnan conceived a plan. "This Redcap will arrive by the main gate," he predicted, "and he should be properly greeted, even welcomed!" In the morning, they would surround him by the river.

Having grown utterly weary of William, Donnan launched the plan in earnest. He sent his youngest brother to steal the Wizard's black cloak; Tavish, a skilled thief, returned quickly, wearing the cape. On his small body, the cape's arms were twice as long as they needed to be, and more then half of it dragged on the ground. He put the hood over his head and made ghoulish sounds, too, acting as if he were a wizard. The three boys laughed, then busied themselves cutting the cape into long strips. The middle brother, with a charming smile, took the cloth to his aunt. Although reluctant to become a pawn in their scheme, she agreed to fold the strips in half and sew them as instructed, and soon completed the task.

The next morning arrived with the brothers by the river. They passed the time by throwing rocks at anything that moved. Soon, a fast moving creature appeared on the horizon, oblivious to becoming their next target. It was storming and the Redcap was slowed by the lighting. He kept getting struck, because his iron boots were such great conductors. The lightning lifted him off the ground, and stood his hair on end. The strikes failed to kill him, but they did make him daft – and as often as he has been struck, this Redcap was nearly senseless!

Donnan raised his eyebrows and smiled as the Redcap spotted the children and rushed to them. The lighting strikes had created a small fire on the Redcap's shirt, and the smoke hastened the drying of his hat. The Redcap needed some more blood! Seizing the opportunity, the boys quoted Bible verses and collected the Redcap's teeth. With the monster distracted as foretold, Donnan struck a deal with him: the teeth would be returned if the Redcap performed one task for the brothers. Tavish then gave the Redcap a dead bird, which he quickly drained of blood. He poured it on his sponge-like hat; replenished, the Redcap scratched the singed hair on his chin and agreed to the deal. And with the leathery face that the children make fun of, and more than a little downtrodden and defeated, the half-charred Redcap slowly entered the castle.

Tavish, meanwhile, returned to his aunt's cottage to gather the cloth now sewn into strips. At the same time, Rory scooped sand from the river. Donnan kept surveillance on William and went over the strategy in his head. The three boys all met at the blacksmiths shop, where it took them a few hours to fill the black cloth with sand and weave it though a metal chain. All three then sneaked into William's bedroom and bound him in a chain of sand while he slept.

In the morning, when William failed to appear, the boys were full of pride, utterly pleased with their latest trick. The community, seeing that William was now safely bound, decided to boil the laird to death. A request was sent by messenger to the King of Scotland, Robert the Bruce, who granted prompt permission – no doubt due to an earlier failed De Soulis plot to assassinate his majesty!

Donnan stood in the castle's courtyard holding up the Redcap's teeth. The creature appeared, and was instructed to build a fire under a cauldron at the circle of standing stones; there William would meet his end. The restrained laird was paraded through the countryside, and, as instructed, the Redcap tended the fire. William was rolled up in a sheet of lead. Several villagers then lifted his heavy body over the cauldron, and dropped him in with a great splash. William screamed before submerging to a slow death. The Redcap fueled the blaze, all the while, stick by stick, until William was reduced to bones; and as he worked, the boys noticed, the Redcap grew weaker and weaker. The heat from the fire had been drying out the Redcap's hat, and before he realized it, death overtook him, too.

Smiles abounded as the kids threw the Redcap's teeth on his corpse and ran off. With glee, the brothers sang and stomped every puddle on the way home. The village was now at peace, a long-awaited harmony finally enveloping the community of Hermitage.

Looking down at Donnan by the river now, I doubt if he and the boys understand the full consequences of all they accomplished. I soon conclude that it does not matter. The community has been granted a new liberty; we were all now in charge of our own destinies. No longer standing in the dark shadows cast by William, the Wizard, and the Redcap, the light of a new day arises on our horizon.

Hermitage Castle

1200's The property belongs to the Dacres who had a stronghold here, but it soon passed to the De Soulis family.
1300's A large keep of four stories is constructed inside a courtyard.
1320 De Soulis family forfeits the castle due to a plot to assassinate King Robert the Bruce (1274-1329). The castle passes to the Grahams of Abercorn, then by marriage to the Douglas family.
1330's William Douglas, The Knight of Liddesdale (c. 1300) played a major role in resisting Edward Balliol and recovers the castle from the English.
1338 Hemitage falls under English control, Sir William Douglas, the Scottish Knight of Liddesdale besieged it, and William holds the castle until 1353 when he is murdered by his godson.
1390's The corner towers are added by the 3rd Earl of Douglas.
1400's A new rectangular wing is added.
1492 Archibald, 5th Earl of Angus, exchanged Hermitage for Bothwell with Patrick Hepburn, Earl of Bothwell. He is encouraged by King James IV (1473-1513).
1566 Hermitage is held by James Hepburn, 4th Earl of Bothwell (1534-1578). After he is badly wounded by Border Reivers (raiders comprised of both English and Scots), James is carried to the castle. Mary, Queen of Scots (1542-1587) rode from Jedburgh to be at Hepburn's side.
1624 The Bothwell Earl, living in poverty and disgrace, dies in Denmark. The castle passes to the Scotts of Buccleuch.
1800's The castle is partly restored and is now in the care of Historic Scotland.

Nine Stone Rig 9" x 12" oil

DUNNOTTAR CASTLE
24" x 30" oil

**Family / Clan Associations:
Lindsay and Keith**

Dunnottar Castle occupies an ancient site upon which major structures have existed since the twelfth century. The stone castle was built in the 1290's by Sir William Keith, Great Marischal. The Keith's are the only Scottish earls to take their title from the office of state rather than their lands; and for over four-hundred years the Keith Earl Marichals had the privilege of overseeing all ceremonial matters at Scottish Court and were responsible for the safety of the Honours of Scotland. In the fifteenth century, Dunnottar's keep was constructed. It was expanded in the sixteenth and seventeenth centuries, only to be besieged in 1652 and destroyed in 1716. The painting renders its appearance in 1998.

Peasants and Maids

A Legend of Dunnottar Castle

The castle is almost hidden in fog and rain; only the silhouette of a large structure can be seen. The sun has dipped below the horizon at the end of the sea. I can feel the wind on my face. There is water aplenty here, in the air, on the ground, rushing down the small gorges; and I can hear the waves of the North Sea crash onto the shore. Moss covers stone and fencepost alike. There appears to be no others present, except for the white sheep that stand motionless, dotting the green countryside. Wet and cold, I turn and go, seeking a warm dry place to spend the night.

I return the next day. The daylight affords a better vision of noble ruins. From a distance, I can see hundreds of birds flying around the castle, and off onto the surrounding cliffs. A long walk brings me to one of the most daunting locations in all of Scotland, where the Dunnottar formation rises some 160 feet above the sea. The crumbling rock of the cliffs allows no access; steep stairs alone grant entry into the multitude of structures, including the chapel, keep, and stables. A seaward side view of the castle reveals several small islands, where seals often bask. There are visitors here today, the isolated locale having sprung to life.

The Keep at Dunnottar

The landward side of the formation features Black Hill. Some 350 years ago, the English Army assembled here in anticipation of invading the great castle. No physical traces remain, only legends of the siege. Oliver Cromwell, the self-proclaimed Lord Protector of England, had ordered the invasion of Scotland after a young Scottish King, Charles II, was hastily crowned at Scone Palace.

Cromwell destroyed the English Crown Jewels; he was eager to do the same to Scotland, and eliminate their icons of monarchy. The Scots, aware of his intentions, chose not to return their precious Honours to Edinburgh Castle, now garrisoned by Cromwell's army; instead, they sent them for safekeeping to Dunnottar Castle. The stone ruins of little color I view today once housed the most coveted, brilliant silver and gold in all Scotland. However, the sword, crown and scepter, made their journey across the kingdom not under army escort or royal parade. Rather, these national treasures were first entrusted to a peasant woman who brought them, concealed, to Dunnottar.

I picture in my mind, Mrs. Drummond, wife of the Minister of Moneydie, a village near Scone, disguising herself as a merchant. With no weapon to protect her, she takes on the task; an act of extraordinary courage, since her capture would have most certainly meant death. She rides through areas heavily patrolled by Cromwell's garrisons, who are under orders to find and seize the Honours. In her comercial pose, she stops at all the markets, until she can deliver to Dunnottar, as chief beneficiary of her native wit, a new shipment of wool - silver and gold!

Once they catch on, the English decide to step up the assault on Dunnottar that had already lasted eight years. A siege engine capable of catapulting large rocks is on its way. The Scots are aware of the impending threat and hasten to devise a new plan for the Honours.

I envision them meeting in the Great Hall, the warmth emanating from the fireplace. It's pheasant for dinner, followed by whisky – testimony to the regularity with which the English fail to keep small ships from supplying Dunnottar by sea. Several complicated plans to move the treasure compete with one another, but the calm voice of Scottish pragmatism prevails: the new plan will be the old plan. And, so the wife of the minister at nearby Kinniff Kirk is recruited for the scheme. The Honours are lowered down a cliff to one of her maids, who simply waits below ostensibly gathering seaweed. Since it is part of a normal routine, the maid garners little notice. She crams the jewels into her basket, covers them with seaweed and simply walks away. Passing through the English line, she freely dispenses coy smiles and shy glances. Then, under the pretense of a commoner's innocence, she disappears over the horizon. Ultimately, her delivery of seaweed, silver, and gold is accepted at Kinniff Kirk, where the Honours are buried in the sanctuary under stone, their security periodically checked.

After a short battle, Dunnottar surrenders. The English Army, eager to confiscate the royal treasure, becomes enraged upon finding that the Honours have once again vanished. They take their revenge by destroying the castle.

So, Cromwell was denied his desire, and Scotland kept the symbols of nationhood. The Honours can be readily viewed today at Edinburgh Castle. Rarer are the stories of courageous peasants and maids, and of how extraordinary treasures were concealed in the most ordinary of things.

The North Sea, Dunnottar Castle

Dunnotttar Castle

400's St. Ninian establishes a church on the site.
681 A fort at the location is besieged by an Orcadian fleet.
900 The site is besieged by Vikings when Donald II (d. 900), the King of Scots is slain.
1100's Parts of the castle date to.
1290 A stone castle is built by Sir William Keith, Great Marsichal of Scotland.
1295-96 After the defeat of John Balliol (1239-1314), Dunnottar fell into the hands of King Edward I (1239-1307). A large English garrison is placed at the stronghold.
1296 The castle is invaded by William Wallace (1272-1305), and the English seek refuge in the sanctuary at the Chapel of St. Ninian. Wallace burns the church along with the English.
1330's Edward III of England (1312- 1377) takes the castle and strengthens it providing one-hundred archers. However, the castle is quickly recaptured by Sir Andrew Moray,
(1297-1338) the Guardian of Scotland.
1382 The Keiths acquire the property, exchanging Struthers in Fife for Dunnottar with Lindsay of the Byres.
1400's A large keep of four stories exists, and ranges of buildings are constructed around a courtyard in the 1500s.
1500's Dunnottar is one of the strongest fortresses in Scotland.
1562 Mary Queen of Scots (1542-1587) stays at the castle.
1594 The castle is captured by Catholic nobles.
1645 The Marquis of Montrose (1612-1650) unsuccessfully besieges the castle; he had hoped to capture the Covenanting 7th Earl Marishal. On retreat, Montrose burns every house in the surrounding parishes.
1650 William, the 9th Earl, entertains the future King Charles II (1630-1685).
1651 The Scottish crown jewels are brought to Dunnottar for safekeeping during Cromwell's invasion of Scotland.
1651 The Army of the English Parliament stand before the castle. They are poised to capture the Honours of Scotland rushed there after the hasty coronation of King Charles II at Scone Palace.
1652 General Lambert (1619-1684) besieged the castle for eight months, he only captures the castle after a mutiny. During the battle, the castle is badly damaged.
1685 Coventer prisoners numbering 167 men and women were packed into a cellar - nine died and twenty-five escaped.
1689 The castle is held for William III and Mary II with many Jacobites imprisoned at the site.
1715 The Earl Marishal allied with the Stewarts during the Jacobite rising. The castle is fortified.
1716 The Duke of Argyll partially destroys Dunnnottar, and in 1718 the castle is further slighted.
2000's The castle is privately owned.

HODDOM CASTLE
8" x 16" oil

Family / Clan Associations:
Carlyle, Herries, Irvines, Halliday, Curruthers, Douglas, Murray, Carnegie, Sharp, and Brooks

---

The land development around the site of the castle dates to the early twelfth century. The current castle was built in 1560 and destroyed ten years later; it was restored and expanded in the seventeenth century. Hoddom's center tower is regarded as one of Scotland's greatest: its walls, nine to fifteen feet thick, rise to over seventy-five feet. The castle was inhabited until 1945 but is now derelict. The painting reproduces its appearance in 2004.

Unintended Consequences

A Legend of Hoddom Castle

Hoddom Castle was one in a chain of strongholds protecting the Lowlands of Scotland. The border region had become coveted territory for England. During the mid 1500's, the kingdom was filled with foreign invaders who entered Scotland from England during the Anglo-Scottish War (or *The Rough Wooing*) of 1543 to 1550. King Henry VIII, of England, was eager for his son, Edward Prince of Wales, to wed the infant Mary Queen of Scots (1542-1587.) Instead, Scotland decided to send their Queen to France, where she was betrothed to Francis, the 17th Dauphin of France. He became King in 1559 before an early death one year later. The sending of Mary to France enraged King Henry VIII of England; he wished to impose a Protestant marriage on Scotland and in so doing an English King. After the death of her French husband, Mary returned to her homeland in August of 1561.

The late 1500's were defined by changing alliances throughout Europe, formed and often broken shortly thereafter. The Kingdom of Scotland was at war with England and the Scottish John, Master of Maxwell, eventually served Queen Mary, but first took actions that led to unintended consequences. The lives of twelve hostages unknowingly became his responsibility. The Lowlands were populated with *Assured Scots* or local lairds (landowners) that had submitted to Henry VIII, including Laird Maxwell head of the clan bearing the same name. John remained uncommitted, but after the Scottish defeat at the 1547 Battle of Pinkie near the River Esk, he joined the English side thus becoming *Assured*.

During February of 1548, Lord Wharton, the English Warden of Scotland, mounted a force against the Scottish James Douglas of nearby Drumlanrig Castle. The raiding party included the *Assured Scots* led by John Maxwell. Wharton distrusted his new leader; before the party embarked he took fifteen of Maxwell's relatives as hostages. It was the eve of battle, and Maxwell had no knowledge of the captives. He arranged a secret meeting with Douglas, and agreed to break his oath with the English and ally with his fellow Scot. In return, he was to receive the hand of fourteen-year-old Agnes Herries in marriage, her dowry included Hoddom Castle which she shared with two sisters.

Lord Warton awoke the next morning to find himself deserted by the Scots. He returned to Dumfries, and then traveled to Carlisle located in northern England; where from its trees, the innocent bodies were displayed. Maxwell's own twelve-year-old nephew was hanged along with eleven others as retribution. Three hostages escaped under unknown circumstances.

John, having miscalculated, immediately challenged Wharton to single combat. Buried in a long written response, Lord Wharton declined. These

Fortifications at Hoddom

actions strengthen John's resolve against the English; Maxwell became a loyal supporter of Queen Mary, and a staunch Scottish patriot.

Maxwell married Agnes and, by so doing, obtained Hoddom Castle. Located directly above the substantial structure is Beacon Hill, where a lone tower began to rise between the years of 1562-65. The building was constructed by Lord Herries (or John Maxwell) as a recompense for the relatives who were lost. He named his tower Repentance, and flanked the door with a serpent and a dove referring to a passage from St. Matthew's Gospel: *Be ye wise as serpents and harmless as doves.*

The Rough Wooing ended with the Treaty of Norham in June of 1551, King Henry VIII died in 1547. Scotland survived its struggles with England, and in 1565, Mary Queen of Scots wedded her second husband, Lord Darnley. He was a King Consort of Scotland, the title symbolic with Darnley's main role to produce an heir to the throne. In 1567, a male child was born to the couple – James VI & I who later becomes King James of Scotland and England.

Hoddom Castle

1200's The property is held by the Carlyles.
1300 and 1400s The property is held by the Herries, then Hallidays, then Carruthers.
1500's Massive L-plan tower house built by the Maxwell, Lord Herries.
1549 Hoddom Castle is held by the Irvines.
1568 The castle is held by the Douglas of Drumlanrig.
1569 The castle is captured by forces loyal to Mary, Queen of Scots (1542-1587).
1570 The English capture the castle and destroy the tower.
1627 Hoddom Castle is rebuilt and acquired by the Murrays of Cockpool.
1653 The castle is owned by the Carnegie, Earls of Southesk.
1690 Hoddom is sold to the Sharp family who extend the castle and add a new wing.
1800's The castle is expanded, and in 1878 the castle is sold to the Brooks.
2000's The castle is privately owned.

Outbuildings, Hoddom Castle

Hoddom Castle

GLAMIS CASTLE
9" x 12" oil

Family / Clan Associations:
Lyon

The area surrounding Glamis Castle was a hunting ground for the royalty of Scotland. Glamis began as a keep in the fourteenth century and was altered in 1500. William Shakespeare visited in 1599, and thereafter the castle's name was forever linked with Macbeth. Glamis underwent further expansion from the seventeenth to the nineteenth century. The painting depicts its appearance in 2006.

Hidden Away

A Legend of Glamis Castle
(Told from the perspective of Jacob Mercer)

I am Father Jacob, the priest assigned to the chapel located within Glamis Castle. My duties require me to tell the secret story of *The Mad Earl*, exclusively for the Earl of Strathmore and Kinghorne's heir on his twenty-first birthday. For decades, I have recounted the tale of the Mad Earl – townspeople call him the Monster of Glamis-in much the same fashion. But now, with his disappearance, everything changed.

Now advanced in years, I write this story, not to expose the family, but so that others may know the truth regarding Thomas Bowes-Lyon. The following account documents my involvement in the mysterious events beginning in 1821.

Thomas's grave is located at the nearby St. Fergus church. His tombstone states he lived and died the same day, and that remains the "official story." I first met Thomas ten years after his "death." Upon my arrival to Glamis, I was led by Malcolm Ogilivy, the castle constable, through a hidden entrance. Thomas' cell was accessed through a removable wooden panel located within the chapel. Down a short tunnel, a cell framed by stone roughly ten foot by fifteen feet held Thomas. He sat before the round opening of an ancient arrow slit. A shackle was secured around one leg with a chain anchored to the wall.

Thomas was a strong but malformed man, his chest like a barrel, his legs small, his arms thick. We stood in silence until he slowly moved his head. For a moment, he peered at us with a haunting gaze. His attention quickly returned to the outside view. The constable introduced us. I smiled and nodded my head, but there was no acknowledgement from him. Malcolm pointed the way out. As we left he mentioned that Thomas' words were few, although he did, at times, speak in simple sentences.

Later that evening, I was instructed by the family to look after his spiritual needs. The castle constable was charged with everything material. Thomas' very existence was a closely guarded secret. Because of his condition, I was advised that he was to be kept where he was, as he was. Years would pass before I disregarded both directives.

In the interim, everything surrounding Thomas continued with methodical routine. Malcolm would bring the meals and was also responsible for his late-night exercise, taken on the castle battlements. Thomas, dragging his chains, lumbered around a section named *Mad Earls Walk*. An occasional sighting by a villager merely added to the legends growing more dramatic with each telling.

Entrusted with the care of his soul, I learned that Thomas was baptized at birth. I could think of nothing else to do but read to him from the Holy Bible. Each day, Thomas would listen to one proverb and every a Sunday a psalm. Eventually, his gaze turned from an outward view and focused on me and the book. We did converse, and I quickly learned that Thomas was not the knave that others made him out to be.

I taught him to read. With his speech improved, he was soon reading to me. My first gift to Thomas was his own bible. In the beginning, he failed to understand and kept trying to give it back to me. Confusion ensued when I would not accept. Eventually, he began reading on his own. Malcolm told me that Thomas had requested more candles, as he put it, "Light to rid the darkness and read the words." During that same discussion, I asked Malcolm if I could exercise Thomas one night a week. He was puzzled and wished to speak with Thomas' father before consent. The next day, I was given the key to Thomas' shackle. That night, Thomas walked without chains on the ground he could view from his makeshift window. More time passed before I was able to talk Malcolm into allowing me full responsibility for Thomas' exercise.

My second gift to the so-called *Monster of Glamis* was a large skeleton key. The castle locksmith made me a copy. Thomas kept it guarded in his pocket. He waited each day for the sun to descend, and could unlock his shackle at will. I watched from my upstairs window as each night Thomas ventured further from the castle. He would always return by morning, in time for Malcolm's breakfast delivery. His shackle re-locked, his gaze, as always, returned to the castle courtyard.

He told me about his explorations, but his favorite trail led to the cemetery at St. Fergus Kirk. He spent hours reading names carved into stones, and underneath those names were often words that matched verses in his bible. His greatest discovery, which he failed to understand, was his own name with the numbers 1821 to 1821 listed below. I explained to him that when words were carved on stone it meant death, but when words were written on paper, touching his book, they represented life.

I was not fully convinced that Thomas comprehended my words, but I was optimistic. After our conversation, the shackle remained locked for weeks. During that time, we spoke little. He then asked me for a chisel and hammer which surprised me. I inquired, "Have you lost the key?"

He shook his head no.

I told him, "Thomas, you have the key to your freedom and can move about at will."

He looked at me with two large eyes and pragmatically stated, "I shall be free indeed."

That was the end of our conversation for the evening, and it was now I who did not understand. A week passed before I brought him the items he requested - the last of my gifts to him.

Upon the setting of the sun, he once again left his cell. Far behind, I followed him. He walked with decisiveness passing though the corner gateway of Glamis Castle, then down the forested trail to the Kirk of St. Fergus. Locating his own grave, he sat in front of his tombstone for hours. The dim moonlight was across his name. Holding out his deformed arm, a long finger repeatedly traced his name, Thomas Bowes-Lyon; it then moved to the year of his birth 1821. He never traced the year of his death. As the hours passed, the moon moved across the sky, changing the shadows on which he relied as a clock or warning of morning. When the shadows grew long, moving up his large chest, and before the darkness overtook his face, he rose, turned towards the castle, and dragging his club foot, made his way back to the cell.

Thomas moved through the chapel, opened the hidden panel, and I soon heard the shackle being locked by his own hand. I checked for many nights after, but he did not leave his cell. During the day, a rhythmic chink, chink, chink sound of steel on stone could sometimes be heard echoing through the castle. The sound originated from Thomas's cell. He first carved the outline of what appeared as a window with an arch on the top. Soon, he added his own name, then the year of his birth, leaving off that of his death. He was copying his own tombstone directly on the wall of his cell. Upon its completion, I witnessed him on several occasions sitting in front of it, putting flesh to stone, running his finger over the words as he had done at St. Fergus.

The days remained unchanged for another two months. It was the 7th day of October, 1848, when the constable awoke me early in the morning with panic displayed on his face. Thomas had vanished! I made my way to the chapel and quickly moved through the small hidden passage. In his cell, an open leg shackle and only one small pamphlet titled, *St. Fergus Kirk*. It was placed directly below the arrow slit where Thomas spent the majority of his time. The work outlined the church's history; the inside cover read: To Thomas, with Love, Charlotte, (his mother.) One of the dog-eared pages explained the life of St. Fergus, how he lived in a cave, the entrance of which had long been lost but it was near the present church. The constable and two others from the village spent the next week looking for Thomas. A month passed with no trace of him ever found. His father, George, related to me that the entrance was to be sealed by brick and Thomas forgotten.

I rushed to take one last look around Thomas's cell. It was as before, although I had missed one thing. An additional date had been engraved into the wall. That line now read 1821 – 686. The current year was 1848, but the new numbers were more finely chiseled than the name above it. The 686 was carved with perfection. Malcolm, who had soon joined me, saw the numbers and questioned me as to what they meant. Not knowing, I shook my head and shrugged my shoulders. Malcolm, Charlotte, and I then watched the stonemason cover the entrance. I once again thought about the 686, and a smile covered my face.

Without giving it away, I slowly retired to my chambers. I opened Thomas's favorite book, Psalms, to read 68:6: *God gives the desolate a home to live in; he leads out the prisoners to prosperity . . .* I had become the priest of Glamis with the commission of keeping Thomas a secret, and after all these years, it was Thomas' own secret that I must now conceal.

Several weeks passed before a new legend was being told at the village pub. The *Mad Earl* was no longer seen pacing, in chains late in the night. Instead, there had been sightings of a beast in the forests surrounding St. Fergus's church. When I was asked about these "visions," my response was, "Mankind has always been haunted by one demon or another; but, like people, visions are not always as they appear."

Later that evening, I traveled to the cemetery at St. Fergus. Like Thomas, I sat in front of his grave reading the inscription, tracing it with my finger. I paid special attention to the date feeling as if I was being watched, I looked around, but located no one. The dates read, 1821-1821. Directly below those numbers and hidden in the grass was the dull shine of metal, the large skeleton key I had made for Thomas years ago. I smiled, placed it in my pocket, and walked the path back to the castle.

I assumed that the key was Thomas' way of saying goodbye, and that I would never see him again. I can only believe that he located St. Fergus' cave, and as his prior home, lives surrounded by rock. He took with him the stone and chisel, and I wonder what he is carving on the walls of his new home. I am comforted by the thought that he found the freedom he so diligently sought. As a reminder of Thomas, I carry the key with me. But I no longer carry the burden of secrecy. Having shared the truth about Thomas, I leave the burdens of the history of Glamis Castle for all to bear.

Glamis Castle

1034 King Malcolm II (d. 1034) is believed to have died at Glamis after being injured at a nearby battle.
1300's A large keep is built that makes up the core of the present castle.
1445 The lands were held by Sir John Lyon, Chancellor of Scotland, who married a daughter of King Robert II (1316-1390). The family is made Lord Glamis.
1500's The structure is altered into an L-plan castle.
1562 Mary, Queen of Scots (1542-1587) visits.
1578 John, 8th Lord of Glamis and Chancellor of Scotland and Keeper of the Great Seal, is killed in a brawl with the Lindsays in Stirling. His brother is one of those involved in the kidnapping of the young King James VI (1566-1625).
1599 William Shakespeare (d. 1616) did research into the area possibly staying at Glamis while he was traveling to Aberdeen, Scotland.
1600 – 1800s Extended with lower wings and round towers.
1606 Patrick, 9th Lord, (1575-1615) was made Earl of Kinghorne.
1677 The Lyon family are made Earls of Strathmore in 1677.
1700 and 1800s The castle develops into a baronial mansion with most of the outer fortifications being demolished and replaced with formal baroque gardens and sculpture walks.
2000's Glamis Castle is privately owned.

View of Glamis

TANTALLON CASTLE
9" x 12" oil

**Family / Clan Associations:
Douglas and Dalrymple**

Tantallon Castle sits atop rocky cliffs overlooking the Firth of Forth. The castle is considered the greatest fortress of Renaissance Scotland. The stonework began in 1350 and was expanded in 1534. The resultant fortress was besieged and destroyed in 1639, and by 1651 reduced to the ruin that it is today. The painting illustrates a view of Tantallon from 2004.

Disruptions

A Legend of Tantallon Castle

Sir Ralph Sadler was an English diplomat and statesman. By 1536, Sadler was made a gentleman of the English King's privy chamber. His knowledge of Scotland was extensive, and he made such an impression that in 1537, Henry VIII sent Sadler from Hampton Court Palace outside of London to Edinburgh, Scotland.

Sadler's mission was to find the truth regarding complaints made by Margaret Tudor against her third husband Lord Methven. The King of Scotland was James V (Margaret's son), and he initially supported Methven in the possession of Margaret's lands; but he soon changed his alliance. Before the divorce was ready for public proclamation, King James V commanded the land transfer to stop. Margaret kept the lands and died in 1541 at Methven.

Sadler's second directive was to investigate the relations between the King of Scotland and the French. Sir Ralph succeeded in helping Margaret and improving the Anglo-Scottish alliance. Because of his achievements, Ralph was able to return to England. However, Henry VIII sent him back to Scotland in 1540. By now, Sadler was a knight and one of two secretaries to King Henry. Sadler's mission was to separate the King of Scotland from Cardinal Beaton, who was the Archbishop of Scotland and a proponent of a Franco-Scottish alliance. Sadler was specifically charged to arrange a marriage between Scotland's new Queen, the baby Mary (Queen of Scots), and Henry's son, Edward Prince of Wales. The arrangement failed and Mary was whisked away to France, where she was betrothed to the Dauphin. He died two years into their marriage, and Mary eventually returned to Scotland as a widow in 1561.

Sadler remained in Edinburgh until his house was besieged by an angry mob. After a narrow miss from musket ball, he moved to the nearby Tantallon Castle. In a letter to Henry VIII, dated 6th November 1513, he remarked, *Temptallon is of suche strenght as I nede not to feare the malice of myne enymeys, and therefore do thinke myself nowe to be out of daunger.* That same year war broke out between Scotland and England. Due to his frequent absences on diplomatic mission away from England, Sadler was unable to carry out his duties as the English Secretary of State and was replaced. He continued to play a role in English-Scottish relations. Under Queen Elizabeth's reign he was once more sent to Scotland with the directive of arranging alliances with the Protestants.

Later, Sadler was selected as one of the commissioners appointed to meet with the Scottish and reach a resolution regarding the imprisoned Mary, Queen of Scots. He found himself twice the warder over the Queen during her time in England, first at Sheffield in 1572, then Wingfield in 1584. He unsuccessfully applied for release from these appointments, but eventually Sadler was one of the council which condemned Mary to death. Her trial was in 1586, and she was sentenced on October 25th. Queen Elizabeth did not

The Firth of Forth

sign the warrant of execution until February 1, 1587. The beheading was carried out a week later at Fotheringhay Castle in England; Mary was buried in Peterborough Cathedral. Her casket was moved to Westminster Abbey in 1612, the same year her son, James became King of Scotland and England. In life, Mary and Elizabeth never met; in death, they rest only a few feet away from one another. Sir Ralph Sadler died in March of 1587, the same year as Mary. At the time, Sir Ralph was celebrated as a trusted English sovereign, soldier, and writer, reputed to be the wealthiest commoner in England. He was buried under an impressive monument at St. Mary's Church in Hertfordshire.

Courtyard

Tantallon, on the Coast

Tantallon Castle

1300's Tantallon is a strong castle consisting of a massive fifty-foot high curtain wall, one of the deepest wells in Scotland, and its own seagate.
1350 The castle is built by William Douglas, 1st Earl of Douglas (1327-1384). Tantallon becomes the seat of the Red Douglas, Earls of Angus.
1402 George Douglas became the 1st Earl of Angus, (1380-1403) A 'Red Douglas' he is captured at the Battle of Homildon Hill where the English defeat the Scots.
Early 1400's James, the 3rd Earl of Angus (1426-1446) used Tantallon to pursue a vendetta against the Black Douglases.
1455 George, 4th Earl of Angus (1424-1462), and King James II (1430-1460) army routed the Black Douglas forces at Arkinholm. He is rewarded with the Lordship of Douglas.
1491 The 5th Earl, Archibald Douglas plotted with King Henry VII (1457-1509) to depose King James IV(1473-1513). The action led the Stewart King to respond with a lengthy siege. James IV led the siege himself from the ship the Flower anchored at nearby Bass Rock.
1482 Archibald, the 5th Earl, known as Bell-the-Cat hanged King James III's (1451-1488) favorites, including Robert Cochrane from the Bridge at Lauder. He then entered into a pact with King Henry VII of England which leads King James IV to siege Tantallon.
1528 The 6th Earl Douglas (1490-1557) had the young King James V (1512-1542) under
arrest for more than two years leading to another siege.
1528 James escapes Tantallon and sieges the castle for twenty days with more the twenty-thousand men. The castle withstands, but he gains Tantallon the following spring with bribery and negotiation.
1543 Tantallon Castle is updated with its central barbican rebuilt in rounded stones capable of withstanding cannonshot.
1566 Mary Queen of Scots (1542-1587) visits.
1639 Covenanters storm the castle in effort to free their co-religionist. They are imprisoned on nearby Bass Rock located in the Firth of Forth.
1650 Moss Troopers, based at the castle damage Cromwell's lines of communication. In 1651, Cromwell sent General Monck (1608-1670) with an army of two-thousand men to attack the castle. The bombardment lasts twelve days destroying much of the castle. The garrison surrenders.
1651 The castle is abandoned, and by 1699 the property is sold to the Dalrymples.
1924 The castle is taken into state care and managed by Historic Scotland.

BLACKNESS CASTLE
9" x 12" oil

**Family / Clan Associations:
Vipont and Crichton**

Blackness Castle was built by Sir George Crichton, who promised King James II that he would build a ship that the English could not sink. Constructed on the edge of the Firth of Forth, the castle has the appearance of a ship. Blackness began in 1440; that structure, burned in 1481 and later restored, was expanded in the 1540's. The keep was strengthened in 1553, and further fortifications were added in the seventeenth century. Besieged in the 1650's, Blackness was restored in 1660. The painting is based on a 2005 view.

Below and Above

A Legend of Blackness Castle
(Told from the perspective of Lundin Wemyss)

The year is 1542, and I, a commoner and prisoner may as well be nameless. Convicted, I am here at Blackness Castle, huddled with my comrades. My crime was stealing bread, and even now there is no silence in my stomach. We poor prisoners are thrown into dungeons, forgotten, with nothing left to do but watch the horizon. An iron grate blocks our hopes and dreams; the only thing it allows is a view of the Firth of Forth. Time moves slowly and is measured by the tide. As if displaced by the setting sun, the water inches its way up the shore, over the rocks, and spills through the grate, splashing on our skin and covering our bare feet. Uninvited, it fills the bottom of the cell. Our bodies attempt to warm themselves, but we shiver with cold. Our only thoughts are for the morning sun, and the scant warmth those few rays will provide. This is the life below.

In the ceiling, a door opens into another world above. The prisoners up there are warm and well-fed. They move about freely; we hear their footsteps from our cell below. Cardinal Beaton, the castle's most famous prisoner, is among them. I know little of him, except that his high station earns him a fireplace, latrine closet, and adequate lighting and ventilation. Above, the Cardinal and friends suffer none of the discomforts we know so well below. The two "prisons," one above the other, symbolize the vast distance in society between those like the Cardinal and those like we, the forgotten.

Blackness Castle

1200 The lands are held by the Viponts.
1400's The lands were acquired by George Crichton, brother of the Chancellor of Scotland. A four-story keep is constructed.
1444 During the reign of King James II (1633-1701), the Douglases sack the castle. The stronghold is quickly regained by the Crichtons.
1453 Sir George Crichton prevents his son, James, from inheriting the property. James captures the castle and imprisons his father until he is forced into surrender by the king.
1481 The castle is burned by an English fleet
1488 The location is the meeting place between King James III (1451-1480) and rebellious nobles.
1537 Work begins to turn the castle into an artillery fort. It becomes one of the most formidable fortresses in Scotland after the keep is heightened.
1540's The castle is fortified by Sir James Hamilton of Finnart (c.1495-1540). He had studied the latest fortifications in Europe, applying the knowledge, the walls of the castle are thickened and port-holes cut for cannons.
1543 Cardinal David Beaton (c. 1495-1540) is imprisoned here.
1548 to 1560 The castle is held by a French garrison.
1568 – 1573 Catholic supporters hold the castle for Mary Queen of Scots (1542-1587), Blackness is won back by the government through intrigue.
1650 The castle is captured by General Monck (1608-1670) during Cromwell's invasion of Scotland, the attack is both by land and sea.
1660 The castle is repaired and used as a prison.
1800's Blackness is greatly altered to hold powder. It becomes the central ammunition depot for Scotland.
1912 The castle is handed over to the state. Between 1926 and 1935, a major restoration is carried out.
2000's Blackness Castle is managed by Historic Scotland.

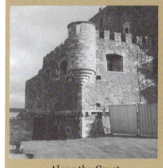
Along the Coast

Entrance to Blackness

SPYNIE PALACE
9" x 12" oil

Bishops Residence
(After the Protestant Reformation – Lindsay)

Today, Spynie Palace lies three miles inland from the sea. In the thirteenth century, however, it sat on a headland jutting into the sea waters of Loch Spynie and was capable of harboring large ships. The Palace originated as a residence for the bishops of Moray. In 1460, David's Keep was added. After the Protestant Reformation in 1560, the palace passed to the Lindsay family. The castle suffered sieges in 1640 and 1645, and by 1688, after the last Roman Catholic Bishops were removed from Scotland, Spynie became derelict. The painting depicts its appearance in 2007.

Signs of Life

A Legend of Spynie Palace

A cool breeze scatters a fine Scottish mist. I am at Spynie Palace, located on Scotland's northern coast. The changing colors of fall highlight a countryside checkered with farms, and the horizon is framed on both sides by encroaching forest. The focal point, located on a hill, is the palace, an ancient ruin that, at its zenith, was a prosperous Bishop's residence, once complete with a cathedral and medieval village. Little of the former glory remains; the area has given itself over to ghosts and legends.

The Moray Valley is noted for large birds, among them cormorants, that dine on 'sea ravens' and other coastal fish. An ancient myth links the fate of these birds to the castle; the story says that as the one goes, so goes the other. Cone-shaped nests, as large as a man, hang from the trees of the now-empty Spynie Loch. The port to the sea was drained of its water years ago. Nature has reclaimed the territory, the thick forest overgrowth creating a barrier and refuge, into which now only those that can fly may enter.

The tower at Spynie overlooks the old loch from the south. A tree-lined path leads to manicured grass and stone monuments that still exude the air of nobility. A massive five-story keep and some smaller walls give testament to a former citadel. A place that once hosted all the manifold activities and business of man is now a preserve of daunting stillness. Matched with the moody weather, Spynie has classic Scottish atmosphere.

The palace was abandoned centuries ago; however, the locals claim signs of life persist, albeit otherworldly. Unexplained lights, joined to unearthly music, are allegedly commonplace, and believed to be the work of bishops who were in league with the Devil. Every Halloween, the claims also say, witches are seen flying to the palace. A phantom piper also resides and plays here. I wonder what the ghostly lion thinks of these solo performances?

My only sighting was of a cormorant flying through the gorge before landing on a branch. I actually heard the massive wings working before seeing the bird, which quickened my pulse. The continued existence of Spynie and the birds gives credence to the old myth. Perhaps nature cannot obliterate the ruins entirely, as long as the birds keep coming. The wildlife, real or imagined, are the rightful Kings and Queens of this Palace.

Spynie Palace

1200 Bishop Richard (1187-1203) builds the Cathedral of Moray at Spynie, where it stayed for twenty-four years before relocating to Elgin in 1224.
1220 Spynie Palace originally had a defensive location on a headland jutting into the sea waters of Loch Spynie.
1460 Bishop David Stewart (d. 1476) strengthens the site by raising a large keep – known as David's Tower.
1493 and 1505 King James IV (1473-1513) visits the Palace. In 1562, there is another royal visit, this time by Mary Queen of Scots (1542-1587).
1567 James Hepburn, the Earl of Bothwell (1534-1578) and 3rd husband of Mary, sheltered here after the defeat at the Battle of Carberry Hill – part of the civil wars surrounding Mary Queen of Scots.
1560 After the Reformation, the Palace and lands were sold to the Lindsays. The castle is subsequently used by Protestant Bishops.
1589 King James VI (1566-1625) stays at the castle.
1640 General Munro (d. 1680) besieges the castle, and Bishop Guthie surrenders it. The castle was held by Innes of Innes and Grant of Ballindalloch, Covenanters against the Gordon Earl of Huntly.
1645 Gordon Earl of Huntly besieges the Spynie Palace while acting for the Marquis of Montrose (1612-1686).
1686 The last resident bishop, Colin Falconer (1623-1686), dies here.
In 1688, all the Bishops, including Hay of Spynie, are removed from office.
1973 Spynie Palace is given over to state care and managed by Historic Scotland.

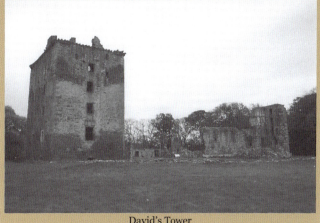

David's Tower

HALLBAR TOWER
12" x 5" oil

**Family / Clan Associations:
De Monfed, Stewart, Maitland, Douglas, and Lockhart**

Hallbar Tower, also known as Braidwood Castle, is located west of the River Clyde. Built in the sixteenth century, the tower was in ruin by 1800; subsequently rebuilt, it was in ruin again by the late twentieth century. Recently restored, Hallbar now exemplifies a structurally unaltered tower house. The painting depicts its appearance in 2004.

Acts of Parliament

A Legend of Hallbar Tower

The Tower of Hallbar occupies a steep hill located above a tranquil brook. The now peaceful Lowlands of Scotland were once rather violent, the volatility stemming from the regularity with which bandits coursed back and forth across the region. Three-hundred years of continuous feuding reached its height in the 1500's. Reivers, fighting men who carried the title of gentleman farmers but were well-versed in guerilla warfare and treachery, were common in the Northumberland, Borders, Dumfries, and Galloway regions of lower Scotland and northern England. Murder, kidnapping, and extortion were common events of the day, and an accepted part of the social system.

Because it conforms to design requirements in an Act of Parliament from Edinburgh in 1535, the Tower is believed to have been built in response to the lawlessness. An edict of King James V directed those with property valued at £100 to construct a tower, thirty-feet square of stone and lime, to protect themselves and their tenants from Border raids. The idea was to strengthen the entire lowland region, and many of these towers were built. What is unique about Hallbar is that it is currently habitable and restored. Most other structures of its nature and age are ruined shells or piles of rubble. In addition, Hallbar has not had a single structural addition through the centuries. Many other such towers became the center of greatly expanded castles.

Hallbar Tower gains mention in a 1581 Act of Parliament ratifying the transfer of the Barony of Braidwood (or the lands associated with the Tower) to Harie Stewart of Gogar, brother to the powerful Earl of Arran. Harie was James VI's chancellor; but on his downfall the Tower passed to his enemy and successor, Lord Maitland, of Thirlestane Castle, located in nearby Berwickshire.

Hallbar Tower
(Previously known as Braidwood Castle)

1000's There is a claim that Hallbar Tower may incorporate an earlier castle.
1326 The Barony of Braidwood is first granted to John de Monford.
1500's The tower house is constructed, originally an Earls of Douglas Stronghold.
1581 Hallbar Tower is acquired by the Stewarts of Gogar, it soon passes to the Maitland of Thirlestane, then to the Douglases.
1681 The castle is purchased by Sir George Lockhart of Lee (c. 1630-1689). His estate adjoined Braidwood (Hallbar) to the south.
1950-60 The Rev. Neville Donaldson, Minister of Glasgow Cathedral lived at Hallbar.
1984 The last tenant left, and the Tower became semi-derelict succumbing to vandalism.
1998 A lease was arranged with the Vivat Trust to restore the Tower and use it as a holiday accommodation.
2000's Hallbar Tower is fully restored.

View from the Brook

DUNSKEY CASTLE
8" x 10" oil

Family / Clan Associations:
Adair, Montgomery, and Blair

Dunskey Castle is perched on an outcrop overlooking the Irish Sea. An older castle on the site burned in 1489. What is in visible ruin today began in 1510. Additions and alterations ensued for the remainder of that century, but the castle was derelict by 1684. The painting depicts its 2008 appearance.

Watchful Eyes

A Legend of Dunskey Castle
(Told from the perspective of Allison Shaw)

From the castle, I view a group of trees that appear to move with unnatural shadows. It is not the branches swaying in the wind but something beyond; and there are times when I hear my own name in a whisper – "Allison." Upon closer inspection, the woods reveal nothing to my eyes and ears. Whoever or whatever it is that lives in those trees, it always vanishes.

It is the summer of 1620. My family, the Montgomerys, has moved to the Dunskey Estate, near the Solway Firth in lower Scotland, purchased from the Adairs by my father Hugh. While remodeling the residence, my quite proper Grandmother and I sense an otherworldly presence. For once, she and I actually agree about something!

The adults, by choice, have confined themselves within the castle walls. But I preferring the freedom and discoveries the countryside offers, have now found the one that called my name. And I and my new friend spend the days exploring the grounds and chasing butterflies. Grandmother Shaw keeps me under close watch from an upstairs window. When she calls my name, I know it is time to come in.

I duck through a back door in an attempt to avoid Grandmother; she always catches up with me in the castle hallways. My happiness depends on clever avoidance, moving from one place to another; but I slowly grind to a stop as she nears. She corners me in the entryway; I am not permitted to run, or scream; and if proper speech is not used, lessons ensue. When she nears, I feel my posture stiffen and my hands immediately lock behind my back. Facial expressions vanish and my eyes become large with dread.

Grandmother begins with the questioning, "Allison, I see you playing and speaking with someone that is not there, who is your friend?" I look down to receive an immediate tap of the chin as she demands, "Well, answer the question?"

In a shaky voice, I respond, "His name is Aberfeldy."

"What does he look like?"

"He is shorter then I, covered in brown hair, his face as flat as a plate with pinhole nostrils, large eyes and ears." I add, "He is here to help."

Puzzled, Grandmother asks, "Help with what?"

I answer, "Our life at this castle."

"Did you ask for this help child?"

Shaking my head, "No, Grandmother."

"Good!" she exclaims, "We are a proud family, and do not accept help which we have not asked for."

There is a silence before her inquisition continues, "Why is it that no one else can see your friend?"

I shrug my shoulders, "I believe that some can see him and others do not." And then I began stepping backward.

Grandmother dismisses me with a promise. "We will revisit the subject."

I bide my time. Waiting at the end of my bed, I am filled with impatience as I count the sound of each closing door. Soon, it will be safe for me to sneak down the hallway. I gently open the door, and with deliberate steps, put very little weight on the creaky floor. As if I had a map in my mind, I remember exactly where to step. Once I hit the stone of the ground floor, my feet move fast, my long red-hair flying back, suspended by the motion. I stop in the kitchen and prepare a bowl of porridge for Aberfeldy; I top it with his favorite, milk and honey. Tonight it is storming, so I rush back to the stairs, slowing my pace before reaching the noisy steps. Walking on my toes back to bed, I drift off to sleep in peace.

By morning, the servants always find an empty bowl. They also wash the dishes without comment, because they wake to fine the house mysteriously and meticulously, cleaned. During breakfast, I daydream about the world outside the castle; after I eat, my desires take me there. Aberfeldy can always be found waiting to explore the grounds, count butterflies, and drink water from the stream. Kneeling down we cup the liquid which pours through our fingers en-route to our lips; but most goes down our fronts. We both find it funny, giggling and rolling upon the ground.

Each evening, Aberfeldy returns to the tree and I enter the castle. After dinner, Grandmother dominates the conservation. Tonight, she is distracted with sewing a brown cloak made of wool and small enough to fit around a baby. Working with a passion to complete the hood, she speaks directly about an evil entity in the house. She drones on about a history of Brownies invading the property, and she clearly believes that one Brownie will attract others. Soon, according to her, we shall be overrun by them! She tells my father that the brown cloak will rid the house of the problem. My father agrees that she should complete the cloak in haste.

Adhering to correct etiquette, I do not speak until asked, but tonight, I break custom. The words pour out of me, informing my elders about all the good things Aberfeldy accomplishes. I am quickly silenced, grabbed and led off to my room. The slamming of the door echoes down the hallway, and I pace in circles. Periodically, I put my ear against the door and I listen for words regarding the Brownie. I hear my Grandmother again present her case for Aberfeldy's removal; but the others seem sympathetic. All the while, she continues stitching the wool. I fear that Aberfeldy's time at the castle is growing short. Alone, in my room, I think about stealing Aberfeldy's new cloak, or grabbing it and throwing it in the fire. I need to talk with Aberfeldy and devise a scheme.

Time moves slowly. I am trapped by it. Impatient, my mind keeps asking, when will they go to sleep? Finally, they are off to bed. I take no caution this night; I run down the stairs, with every step a loud creak. Searching the estate for Aberfeldy, I fail to locate him anywhere. Outside, the night air is fresh with a chill causing goose bumps on my skin. The small stream near the castle flows violently after a recent rain. I do not venture far into the foggy darkness, and look back frequently to keep the castle in sight. My steps slow; I have gone as far as courage will take me. In desperation, I yell for Aberfeldy. He calls my name, and his voice calms my heart. I look to him saying, "I don't want you to go. Grandmother is making you a cloak. She tells me that you are a Brownie, and once it is complete you must leave. Is that true?"

Aberfeldy holds out a closed fist, his long fingers unfolding one by one. Palm open, he displays a small rock necklace on leather band, and responds, "When the cloak is finished, I will vanish. This is for you, my friend."

Tears flow down my face and I ask, "Where will you go?"

"Where I am needed, I will find another home. We normally stay with the same family; but we must go when we are no longer wanted." With squinting eyes, he looks toward the castle. "Allison, the old one is watching us."

I circle around to see Grandmother peering out of her upstairs window; as I turn back, Aberfeldy is gone. I wipe my tears, put on the necklace from Aberfeldy, and walk back to the castle. With contempt, I stare at Grandmother the entire way. Our eyes lock, I never look down, not even once.

Grandmother remains awake late into the night completing the cloak, then leaves it in the kitchen. Sitting at my window, I watch Aberfeldy carry it out of the castle. His ears, normally perky and upright, are pasted to the side of his head. With sadness, he looks up at me, buttons up his new cloak, and then disappears into the darkness.

I later think, *Grandmother has made this place like herself, vacant and lonely, intact but yet a hollow shell.* Life at Dunskey is more difficult. I watch the butterflies; but no longer have the desire to chase them. I hold Aberfeldy's rock and often look towards his tree.

There is so much more work to be done now that Aberfeldy is gone. My time is spent cleaning the castle. This mansion has taken on a sorry new character. Noises punctuate the night. Items come up missing. Doors lock without human intervention. A servant girl's child falls to his death through a broken window. The ill and mad flock to the grounds in hopes of being healed in the cave by the shore. It is a different world now, except that my life continues under Grandmother's watchful eye. I no longer want to leave my room.

Another day passes, and I lay in my bed staring at the ceiling. Unable to sleep, I long for the night air. Stepping out of my bed, I reach the door and put my hand on the knob. I listen for a few minutes, crack open the door enough to peer down the hall before leaving the castle. The sea breeze adds freshness to the air and brings me to life. There are no eyes on me this evening; I walk far from the castle. Upon return, I expect Grandmother to be there. Though the curtain is pulled back, the window is empty. I am troubled, and ponder the meaning of her absence. Surprising myself by my feelings, I actually miss her.

Once inside, I find her motionless, slumped in a chair by the fireplace. I touch her cold hand and look into her face. It is the first time I ever really looked at her; and in that moment I see an older reflection of myself. Her eyes are closed, never again to open. I back away and scream for my father.

After funerals for Grandmother and for the servant's baby, my life returns to routine. I continue my nightly escapes and become free in the night air. The unexplained noises in the castle grow more infrequent, and there are times that I believe I see glimpses of a Brownie in the shadows. Then one night, she appeared. This Browine has the look of a pauper. I later learned that Aberfeldy sent her to serve over the family. She is disheveled and either did not realize it or did not care. I thought, *we will need to work on that*. Her greatest possession is a little bag hanging on a stick, her shoulder the fulcrum, her hand the pivot. I wonder what is in it as she tells me her name, "Cathella," she quickly adds, "I will stay as long as I am wanted."

"Where is Aberfeldy?"

"He has gone to the Castle of St. John to serve the Adairs of Kilhilt. They are the family that originally built this castle. So, he is not far from here."

I ask, "What is in your bag?"

"Oh, little rocks with leather ropes. I make necklaces out them, I made the one on your neck."

I smile and point to the tree, showing Cathella where the Brownies live. I dismiss myself, "I will see you in the morning." While walking back to the castle, I think about how the loses of family and friends have changed me. I feel much older than my present age of thirteen. Aberfeldy came to take care of me, and now, I am taking care of Cathella.

The next morning I skip breakfast. My feet carry me out of the castle. It is a rare day of sun; the light reveals beauty. Although I miss Aberfeldy, I enjoy helping Cathella. Today I am showing her how to catch butterflies; tomorrow, we may work on her hair. I watch as she holds out her hand, scoops one up, its legs forming a claw around her finger, and its wings flapping gently. A smiling Cathella looks into its eyes. In a moment, the butterfly turns loose of her finger and flies away.

Dunskey Castle

1489 An older castle on the site was burned by MacDulloch of Myrton in retaliation for the murder of Dionysius of Hamilton by William Adair of Dunskey.
c. 1510 A tower house of four stories is constructed. The stronghold is started by the Adairs of Kilhilt.
1620 Dunskey Castle is sold to Hugh Montgomery (1560-1636).
1660's The castle is sold to John Blair, Minister of Portpatrick.
By 1684 Dunskey is a ruin.
2000's The castle is privately owned.

View from Portpatrick 10" x 8" oil

CULZEAN CASTLE
9" x 12" oil

Family / Clan Associations:
Kennedy

Culzean Castle overlooks the Ayrshire coast. What began in the sixteenth century as a simple keep received steady improvement from 1762 to 1775. The castle, in its current state, is considered a masterpiece of Scottish Gothic Revival; it dates from the remodeling, during the years 1777-1792, for which the famous Scottish architect Robert Adam was commissioned, at a price that bankrupted Culzean's owner, the Earl of Cassilis. The painting is based on its appearance in 2006.

Revealed

A Legend of Culzean Castle

During the eighteenth century, smuggling, or the Running Trade, was widespread at Culzean Cove and the Ayrshire Coast of western Scotland. The castle and the caves are in close proximity to the Isle of Man (a self-governing crown dependency in the Irish Sea). The Earl of Man, Thomas, was an ardent Jacobite and supported returning the Stuart dynasty to power, as did most of his smuggling dynasty. Their activities, in defiance of the Hanoverian government, proved highly profitable. Goods, those either forbidden or attracting high duties, could be legally imported on payment of small duties to the Lord of Man and then shipped into England.

Records of 1747 show Archibald Kennedy, an estate factor, and Sir Thomas Kennedy conducted business from Culzean. In fact, Archibald was in partnership with George Moore who is remembered as one of the most successful Manxmen smugglers. Items traded included: Lisbon (port), rum, spirits, tobacco, tea, and whisky. For centuries, the Culzean Kennedys and others on the estate were directly involved in smuggling or turned a blind eye to it in exchange for a share in the profits.

Culzean Castle's origins date to the fifteenth century. By 1777, a neo-gothic mansion crowned the cliffs that rise from the Firth of Clyde. The extravagance of the edifice above ground conceals the complexity below. Two cave systems are present under the castle. They are entered through impressive fortifications of arched stone facades complete with walls, doors, and windows. With grotto-like appearance, these entrances face the sea and are easily accessible from shore.

Three tunnels comprise the labyrinth. The first cave system is entered directly above sea level, another doorway is higher. Two separate caves run over one-hundred feet. Once inside, caverns open to rooms as large as forty feet wide, and heights reaching up to thirty-five feet. A third entrance is nearby, located underneath the castle stables. This cave has two entrances, only a few yards apart, which converge into one tunnel. It stretches inward over 250 feet, and has a maximum height and width of twenty feet. Passage is difficult in places, and areas of both caverns move with large spiders and contain human remains.

Throughout the ages, the caves have served as shelter, sanctuary, and tomb. The myths abound. Fairies are believed to use them on moonlight nights for dancing halls. A bagpiper once entered to chase out the ghosts; he was never seen again. His pipes were last heard at a spot called Pipers Brae about half a mile from the castle.

The last and most interesting use of the caves at Culzean was for the protection and storage of prohibited goods. Although by the 1760's smuggling activities along the Ayrshire coast were diminished due to the increased

Castle Entrance

diligence of revenue officers, the Manxmen continued to take advantage of unrestricted trade until 1765, when the crown of England regained control by purchasing the island. This effectively ended the trade freedom granted to the island by King Henry IV to Sir John Stanley in 1405. Sir Thomas Kennedy, the 9th Earl of Cassillis, did not want to get caught breaking the law, so he halted the smuggling operation at Culzean. Thomas then diversified into the slave trade to increase estate income.

Thomas' heir, David Kennedy, hired the famous Scottish Architect, Robert Adam, to transform Culzean Castle. The remodel bankrupted David, but the fashionable country seat on display today is the product of those efforts. By the twentieth century, the caves were unused and largely forgotten.

Culzean Castle
(Pronounced "cull-ANE")

1100's The lands are the property of the Kennedy's, they are one of Scotland's oldest families.
1762-1775 Sir Thomas Kennedy (1733-1775) repairs the old castle and adds a new wing.
1777 David, 10th Earl Cassillis (1734-1792) commissions architect Robert Adam (1728-1792) to build the finest grand mansion in the kingdom. David bankrupts himself in the process.
1777-1792 The present mansion is built incorporating part of a 1500's L-plan tower house.
1945 The castle is managed by the National Trust for Scotland.
1945 The use of the top floor is granted to General Dwight Eisenhower (1890-1969). He visits in 1950 as President of the U.S.A.

The Front, Culzean Castle

The Last of Fall, Culzean Estate

Appendices

APPENDIX 1
MAJOR CLANS OF SCOTLAND

APPENDIX 2
THE ROYAL DYNASTIES AND MONARCHS OF SCOTLAND

House of Alpin

843-60 Kenneth I MacAlpine
860-63 Donald I
863-77 Constantine
877-78 Aed
878-89 Eochaid
889-900 Donald II
900-42 Constantine II
942-50 Malcolm I
950-62 Indulf
962-67 Dubh
967-71 Colin or Cuilean
971-95 Kenneth II
995-97 Constantine III
997-1005 Kenneth III
1005-34 Malcolm II
1034-40 Duncan I
1040-57 MacBeth
1057-58 Lulach

House of Dunkeld

1058-93 Malcolm III (Ceann Mor)
1093-94 Duncan II
1093-94 Donald Ban
1094 Duncan II
1094-97 Edmund
1097-1107 Edgar
1107-24 Alexander I
1124-53 David I
1153-65 Malcolm IV, The Maiden
1165-1214 William the Lion
1214-49 Alexander II
1249-86 Alexander III
1286-90 Margaret, The Maid of Norway
1292-96 John Balliol

House of Bruce

1306-29 Robert I, The Bruce
1329-71 David II

House of Stewart

1371-89 Robert II
1389-1406 Robert III
1406-37 James I
1437-60 James II
1460-88 James III
1488-1513 James IV
1513-42 James V

House of Stuart

1542-67 Mary Queen of Scots
1567-1625 James VI and James I of England
1625-49 Charles I
1649-60 The Commonwealth
1660-85 Charles II
1685-89 James II- Jacobite line
1689-1702 William and Mary
1702-14 Anne

1707-The Act of Union
The Act joined the Kingdom of England with the Kingdom of Scotland to form the single Kingdom of Great Britian

House of Hanover

1714-27 George I
1727-60 George II
1760-1820 George III
1820-30 George IV
1830-37 William IV
1837-1901 Victoria

House of Saxe-Coburg-Gotha

1901-1910 Edward VII

House of Windsor

1910-36 George V
1936 Edward VIII
1936-52 George VI
1952- Elizabeth II

Glossary

Anglo-Saxon or Anglo-Saxons: A term applied to the Germanic peoples who migrated to Great Britian in the fifth and sixth centuries. The Benedictine monk, Bede (d. 735), identified Anglo-Saxons as the descendants of Germanic tribes.

Anglo-Scottish: A label applied to people and things that are identified with both England and Scotland. Often used in reference to people born in, raised in, or long-term residents of England who have significant Scottish ancestry, or born and brought up in Scotland with English ancestry.

Anglo-Norman: Descendants of Normans who ruled England following the Norman Conquest by William of Normandy in 1066.

Anwan: An ancient mythical land.

Auld Alliance: Refers to a series of treaties, offensive and defensive in nature, between Scotland and France - until 1326 also Norway. The treatise are against England. The first such agreement was signed in Paris on 23 October 1295 then ratified at Dunfermline the following February. During the reign of John Balliol (1292-1296) and Philip the Fair (1285-1314), it was renewed on several subsequent occasions affecting Franco-Scottish and English affairs until the Treaty of Edinburgh (1560.)

Barony: Land and corresponding area of influence held by a Baron – a nobleman who belongs to the lowest rank of British nobility.

Betrothed: A formal contract blessed by a religious authority. Betrothed couples were legally regarded as husband and wife even before their wedding and physical union. A Betrothal was as binding as marriage and a divorce was necessary to terminate the contract.

Brownie: A legendary creature popular in folklore around Scotland and England.

Castle: Normally the residence, defensive in nature, of a monarch or noble that commanded a specific territory.

Clan: A group of people united by kinship and descended from a common ancestor. This kinship may be actual or symbolic but serves as the basis of unity. Scottish clans consist of both "Native Men," or those that had a direct blood relationship with the chief and "Broken Men" who were individuals that sought protection from the clan. Also see *Sept*.

Covenanters: An adherent of the National Covenant who, by agreement, pledged to uphold Presbyterianism in Scotland.

Dower House: A moderately large house on an estate which is occupied by the widow of the late owner. Other widows may reside in the house. The widow is refered to as the Dowager.

Dowry: The money, goods, or estate that a woman brings to her husband in marriage.

Elfland: A mythical geographical location where elves or fairies live.

Fairy: A type of legendary creature, generally conceived as having a diminutive human form and possessing magical powers with which they intervene in human affairs.

Feudalism: A political system composed of a set of reciprocal legal and military obligations among the warrior nobility. The system is based on the three key concepts of lords, vassals, and fiefs. The term feudalism and the system it describes were not conceived of as a formal political system by the European people living in the Medieval Period (400s – 1400s.) Also see *Fief, Lord, Serf, and Vassals*.

Fiefs: Land in medieval times was sectioned into fiefs which was a trust, rather than an ownership. The oldest son could inherit the fief. The term carries with it more than land; each section was a complete unit comprised of one village, huts for the serfs, the manor house or castle with areas set aside to grow, feed, or catch food - the fields, pasture land, and woods. Also see *Feudalism*.

Garret: The attic: a room at the top of a house or castle, directly below the roof.

Gowrie Conspiracy: A much disputed episode during the reign of James VI. Alexander Ruthven and his brother, the Earl of Gowrie enticed the king to come to Gowrie House in Perth on August 5th, 1600 for the purpose of murdering or kidnapping him. During the scuffle both Ruthven and Gowrie perished.

Jacobite: A supporter of James II and VII and his descendents in the restoration of the Stuart kings to the thrones of England, Scotland, and Ireland. The Jacobite Risings were a series of uprisings, rebellions, and wars occurring between 1689-1746.

Jester: A person employed to tell jokes and provide general entertainment. Typically hired by European monarchs, Jesters are thought to have worn brightly colored clothes and eccentric hats.

Laird: A member of the gentry and a heritable title in Scotland, granted to the owners of landed estates in Scotland and may carry certain local or feudal rights. The word Laird comes from the shortened form of 'lavered', which is an old Scottish word deriving from an Anglo-Saxon term meaning 'Lord.'

Lord: A title with various meanings. It can denote a prince or a feudal superior (especially a feudal tenant who holds directly from the king, i.e., a baron). The title is most used in connection with peerage. Five ranks of peer exist in the United Kingdom, in descending order they are: duke, marquess, earl, viscount, and baron. The title 'Lord' is used most often by barons.

Manxmen: A citizen of the Isle of Man that is located in the Irish Sea.

Minch: The sea channel in northwestern Scotland. It separates the Outer Hebrides from the Inner Hebrides and the mainland. It is divided into the Minch and the Little Minch.

Morvan: A mythical Gaelic land located in high mountain places throughout Scotland.

Palace: A royal residence or the home of a head of state or some other high-ranking dignitary. In many parts of Europe, the term is also applied to relatively large buildings built as private aritocratic mansions.

Peasants: The only outsiders allowed to live on a fief. These tenants received protection and the use of a small piece of land on which to build a home in exchange for work.

Peerage: A noble rank: the rank, status, or title of a nobleman or noblewoman. Five ranks of peer exist in the United Kingdom, in descending order they are: duke, marquess, earl, viscount, and baron. The title lord is used most often by barons.

The House of Plantagenet: A royal house founded by Henry II of England, son of Geoffrey V of Anjou. Plantagenet kings first ruled the Kingdom of England in the 12th century. Plantagenet was the family name of a line of English kings from Henry II 1145 to Richard III 1485.

Picts: A confederation of tribes living in what was later to become eastern and northern Scotland from before the Roman conquest of Britain until the 10th century. They spoke an extinct Pictish language.

Peel: A small tower, fort, or castle, also used to refer to a keep.

Regeant of Scotland: In a monarchy, the regeant normally rules due to the actual monarch's absence, incapacity, or minority.

Robin Redcap: A type of imaginary malevolent murderous creature found in Border Folklore. They are said to inhabit ruined castles located along the border between England and Scotland.

Scotch-Irish or Scots-Irish: Refers to inhabitants of the United States and, by some, of Canada who are of Ulster Scottish descent (Ulster is a geographical area of Northern Ireland). The term may be qualified as in Scots-Irish American or American of Scots-Irish ancestry. Today, people in the British Isles of a similar ethnicity or ancestry usually call themselves Ulster Scots.

Scoto-Norman or Scotto-Norman, Franco-Scottish, Franco-Gaelic: A term used to described people, families, institutions and archaeological artifacts that are partly Scottish and partly Norman. The term is used to refer to people or things of Norman, Anglo-Norman, French or even Flemish origin, but are associated with Scotland in the Middle Ages. It is also used for any of these things when they exhibit syncretism between French or Anglo-French culture on the one hand, and Gaelic culture on the other. An example would be Robert the Bruce, who had a dual Norman-Gaelic heritage.

Sennachies: A Scottish story-teller versed in reciting genealogies, history, legends, and tales.

Sept: A word for the division of a clan. Often a family line was allied with a larger clan. In this way, smaller clans gained legitimacy and protection. Larger clans were able to form allegiances with several septs for military advantage and political gain. Each major clan typically has a number of septs, with each sept carrying its own surname. Septs have the right to wear the clan tartan, although they sometimes have their own. Related septs, or individual familial lines that subdivided were also common in Scotland. Also see *Clan*.

Serf: Under feudalism, it was a condition of bondage or modified slavery which developed primarily during the High Middle Ages (1000-1300) in Europe. Serfdom was the enforced labour of people on the fields of landowners, in return for protection and the right to work on their leased fields. Also see *Feudalism*.

Stewart and Stuart: The name Stewart was originally adopted as the family surname. During the 16th century, the name underwent a change when the French spelling Stuart was adopted. The change occurs when Mary Queen of Scots uses the spelling to ensure the correct pronunciation of the Scottish name Stewart while she was living in France.

Tinchel: A circle of hunters that surround an open space and gradually close in, bringing a number of deer and other game within a narrow compass.

Wherry: A type of boat used for carrying cargo and passengers.

Vassals: Associated with the feudal system, whereby a person granted the use of land, in return for rendering homage, fealty (loyalty sworn to a feudal lord by a vassal or tenant), and usually military service or its equivalent to a Lord or other superior.

Bibliography
(Selected Further Reading)

Aries Philippe, and Duby, Georges, eds. *A History of Private Life: Revelations of the Medieval World*. Cambridge, Massachusetts: The Belknap Press of Harvard University Press, 1988.

Boswell, James. *The Journal of a Tour to the Hebrides with Samuel Johnson*. Glasgow: First published in 1785.

Cantlie, Hugh. *Ancestral Castles of Scotland*. London: Collins and Brown, 1992.

Cavendish, Richard, ed. *Legends of the World*. New York: Barnes & Noble Books, 1994.

Chadwick, Nora K. *Celtic Britain*, London: Thames and Hudson, 1967.

Coventry, Martin. *Castles of the Clans*, Edinburgh: Goblinshead, 2008.

----------------------. *The Castles of Scotland*, Edinburgh: Birlinn Ltd., 2006.

Coventry, Martin and Joyce Miller. *Churches and Abbeys of Scotland*, Musselburgh: Goblinshead, 2003.

Dargie, Richard Lewis Campbell. *Scottish Castles and Fortifications*, Berks: GWPublishing 2004.

George Way of Plean and Romilly Squire. *Scottish Clan & Family Encyclopedia*, New York: Barns and Noble Books, 1999.

Grant, Niel. *Scottish Clans and Tartans*, Connecticut: The Lyons Press, 2000.

Harris, Nathaniel. *The Heritage of Scotland: A Cultural History of Scotland & Its People*, London: Bounty Books, 2000.

Hislop, Malcolm. *Medieval Masons*, Buckinghamshire: Shire Publications, 2000.

Hollister, Warren C., Joe W. Leedom, Marc A. Meyer, and David S. Spear. *Medieval Europe: A Short Sourcebook*, New York: McGraw Hill, 1997.

Jarvie, Gordon, ed. *Scottish Folk and Fairy Tales*, London: Penguin Group, 1997.

Maritine, Roddy. *Scottish Clan and Family Names: Their Arms, Origins and Tartans*, Edinburgh: Mainstream Publishing Co., 1992.

Menzies, Gordon. *In Search of Scotland*, Maryland: Roberts Rinehart, 2001.

Montgomery-Massinberd, Hugh and Sykes, Christopher Simon. *Great Houses of Scotland*, Leicester: Bookmark Ltd., 2005.

Price, David. *A Short History of Scotland*, Glasgow: William Blackwood and Sons, 1911.

Reid, Stuart. *Castles and Tower Houses of the Scottish Clans 1450-1650*, Oxford: Osprey Publishing, 2006.

Tabraham, Chris. *Castles of Scotland: A Voyage Through the Centuries*, London: BT Batsford, 2005.

The Scottish Tartans with the Badges, Arms, Slogans, etc. of the Clans, Glasgow, Millar & Lang, c. 1930.

The Scottish Tartans with the Badges, Arms, Slogans, etc. of the Clans, Rentons Ltd., Edinburgh, 1920.

Tranter, Nigel. *Tales and Traditions of Scottish Castles*, Glasgow: Neil Wilson Publishing, 1996.

Wilson, Alan J., Des Brogan, and Frank McGrail. *Ghostly Tales & Sinister Stories of Old Edinburgh*, Edinburgh: Mainstream Publishing, 2005.

Wilson, Barbara Ker. *Scottish Folk-Tales and Legends*, New York: Oxford Press, 1989.

Zaczek, Iain and Phillips, Charles *The Complete Book of Tartan*, Edinburgh: Lomond Press, 2004.

Guidebooks are available for most castles and manor houses open to the public.

INDEX
FAMILY NAME / CLAN INDEX

Bishops Castle: Spynie Palace 116
Royal Castles: Doune Castle 46, Edinburgh Castle 63 and Stirling Castle 63

Adair - Dunskey Castle, 120
Bisset - Kilravock Castle, 49
Blair - Dunskey Castle, 120
Campbell - Dunstaffnage Castle, 29
Campbell – Stalker Castle, 52
Campbell - Mingary Castle, 40
Campbell of Argyll - Duart Castle, 26
Campbell of Breadalbane - Kilchurn Castle, 54
Carlyle - Hoddom Castle, 104
Carnegie - Hoddom Castle, 104
Carruthers - Hoddom Castle, 104
Cathcart - Kisimul Castle, 12
Comyn - Blair Castle, 37
Comyn - Urquhart Castle, 32
Crichton - Blackness Castle, 114
Dacre - Hermitage Castle, 97
Dalyrymple - Tantallon Castle, 111
Douglas - Aberdour Castle, 94
Douglas - Hallbar Tower, 118
Douglas - Tantallon Castle, 111
Douglas - Threave Castle, 68
Douglas - Traquair House, 78
Douglas - Hermitage Castle, 97
Durward - Urquhart Castle, 32
Erskine - Braemar Castle, 58
Farquharson - Braemar Castle, 58
Forbes - Craigievar Castle, 56
Gordon - Fyvie Castle, 80
Gordon - Kisimul Castle, 12
Gordon - Threave Castle, 68
Gordon - Huntly Castle, 22
Graham - Hermitage Castle, 97
Grant - Urquhart Castle, 32
Halliday - Hoddom Castle, 104
Hepburn - Hermitage Castle, 97
Herries - Hoddom Castle, 104
Hume - Hume Castle, 91
Irvine - Hoddom Castle, 104
Keith - Dunnottar Castle, 101
Kennedy - Culzean Castle, 124
Leith - Fyvie Castle, 80

Leslie - Mingary Castle, 40
Lindsay - Dunnottar Castle, 101
Lindsay - Fyvie Castle, 80
Lockhart - Hallbar Tower, 118
Lyon - Glamis Castle, 107
MacDonald - Mingary Castle, 40
MacDonald of Clan Ranald – Castle Tioram, 24
MacDougall - Dunstaffnage Castle, 29
MacDuff - Huntly Castle, 22
MacGregor - Kilchurn Castle, 54
MacIans - Mingary Castle, 40
Mackenzie - Eilean Donan Castle, 34
Macleans - Duart Castle, 26
Macleod - Dunvegan Castle, 43
MacNeil - Kisimul Castle, 12
Macrae - Eilean Donan Castle, 34
Maitland - Hallbar Tower, 118
Maxwell - Hoddom Castle, 104
Maxwell - Threave Castle, 68
Meldrum - Fyvie Castle, 80
Montgomery - Dunskey Castle, 120
Mortimer - Aberdour Castle, 94
Mortimer - Craigievar Castle, 56
Murray - Hoddom Castle, 104
Murray - Scone Palace, 19
Murray of Atholl - Blair Castle, 37
Preston - Fyvie Castle, 80
Rose - Kilravock Castle, 49
Ruthven - Scone Palace, 19
Scott - Hermitage Castle, 97
Seton - Fyvie Castle, 80
Sharp - Hoddom Castle, 104
Soulis - Hermitage Castle, 97
Stewart - Hermitage Castle, 97
Stewart - Traquair House, 78
Stewart - Hallbar Tower, 118
Stewart of Atholl - Blair Castle, 37
Stewart of Appin - Stalker Castle, 52
Urquhart - Urquhart Castle, 32
Vipont - Blackness Castle, 114
Watson - Aberdour Castle, 94

Index

A

Abbey at Scone 20
Abbey of Crosseguel 90
Aberdeen 57
Aberdour Castle 94, 96
Aberfeldy 121, 122
Act of Parliament 119
Act of Union 8, 64
Adair 120
Adairs of Kilhilt 123
Adam, Robert 126
Airdchartdan 33
Airdrie 84
Alan of Galloway 17
Alan Stewart 90
Alba 8, 64
Alexander 3rd Lord of Home 92
Alexander III 17, 81
Alexander of Lorne 30
Alford 57
Allan, the chief of Clanranald 25
Angles 64
Anglo-Norman 17
Anglo-Saxons 64
Anglo-Scottish alliance 112
Anglo-Scottish War 105
Antonine's Wall 8, 20, 64
Antrim, Northern Ireland 6
Anwan 44
Apostle of the Picts 33
Arbroath 20
Arbroath Abbey 84, 86
Archbishop of Scotland 112
Archbishop of St. Andrews 92
Ardnamurchan Point 25
Argyll 92
Assured Scots 105
Atlantic Ocean 8, 41, 64

Auchenlick House 7
Auld Alliance 75, 92
Ayrshire Coast 125, 126

B

Banxton Hill 92
Bar-le-duc in Lorraine, France 75
Barony of Braidwood 119
Battle of Bannockburn 81
Battle of Culloden 50, 61
Battle of Flooden 48, 92
Battle of Happrew 85
Battle of Largs 17
Battle of Methven 30, 85
Battle of Pinkie 105
Battle of Pinkie Cleugh 53
Battle of Roslin 85
Battle of Sauchceburoun 48
Battle of Sheriffmuir 25
Battle of Solway Moss 76
Beacon Hill 106
Bear Gates 79
Bell, John 57
Ben Cruichan 30
Ben Nevis 8
Berwick 8
Berwickshire 119
Bisset 49
Blackness Castle 114, 115
The Black Dinner 73
Black Friday 92
Black Hill 102
Black Knight of Rhodes 55
Blair 37, 38, 39, 120, 123
Blair Castle 37, 38, 39
Bonnie Prince Charlie 21, 31, 39, 45, 50, 77, 79
Borders 119
Borthwick 92
Boswell, James 7
Bowes-Lyon, Thomas 108, 109
Braemar 60

Braemar Castle 58, 59, 60, 62
Braemar Games 61
Braemar Highland Society 61
Branxton Hill 92
Bridge of Awe 30
Britannia 8, 64
Britons 64
Brooks 104
Bruce, Robert The 17, 18, 19, 21, 23, 30, 31, 33, 36, 42, 45, 73, 76, 77, 82, 85, 86, 96, 100, 132
Bruce, Marjorie 76
Bruce's plaid 30
Burns, Robert 50

C

Caerlaverock Castle 85
Caithness 53
Caledonia 8, 64
Campbell 25, 28, 29, 30, 31, 40, 52, 53, 54, 55, 90
Campbell of Argyll 26
Campbell of Glenorchy 54
Campbell, Margaret 55
Campbell, Sir Collin 55
Captain of Clanranald 25
Cardinal Beaton 112, 115
Carlisle 105
Carlyle 104
Carnegie 104
Castlebay 14, 15
Castle of St. John 123
Castle Stalker 3, 52, 53
Castle Tioram 24
Cathcart 12
Celtic 8
Charles II 102
Charles Stewart 79
Cistercian Priory 81
Clanranald 25
Clan Campbell 25, 30, 53, 55
Clan Grant 50

Clan MacDougall 30
Clan MacGregor 55
Clan Maclean 41
Clan Macleod 43
Clan MacNab 30
Comorants 117
Comyn 19, 21, 23, 30, 32, 37, 39, 85, 86
Comyn, John (The Red Comyn) 30, 85, 86
Comyn, John II 86
Comyn, John III 85
Covenanters 50
Craig 78
Craigievar Castle 56, 57
Crauford, Sir Ranald 85
Crawford 92
Crichton 70, 72, 114
Cromwell 102, 103
Cromwell, Oliver 102
Culzean Castle 124, 125, 126
Culzean Cove 125
Curruthers 104
Curse of Scotland 48

D

Dacre 97
Dacre's Calvary 92
Dalrymple 111
Danzig Willie 57
Dauphin of France, 17th 77, 105, 112
David, the Duke of Rothesay 18
Declaration of Arbroath 86
DeSoulis 97
Devon 23
De Guise, Mary 75
De Monfed 118
Donald of the Hammer 53
Douglas 68, 70, 78, 83, 94, 97, 104, 105, 111, 118
Douglas, David 70

Douglas, James 105
Douglas, William 69
Doune Castle 46, 47, 48
Drumlanrig Castle 105
Duart Castle 26
Duke of Albany 48
Duke of Cumberland 50
Duke of Fife 61
Dumfries 30, 105, 119
Dumfries Church 86
Dundee, Scotland 6
Dunfermline 85
Dunnottar Castle 101, 102, 103
Dunskey Castle 120, 121, 122
Dunstaffnage Castle 20, 29, 30, 31
Dunure Castle 87
Dunvegan Castle 43, 44, 45
Durward 32

E

Earls and Marquises of Bute 18
Earls of Atholl 38
Earl of Argyll, Colin Campbell 31
Earl of Arran 119
Earl of Douglas, 6th 70, 105
Earl of Man 125
Earl of Mar 25
Earl of Pembroke 30
Earl of Strathmore and Kinghorne's heir 108
Edinburgh 23, 92, 93, 95, 112, 119
Edinburgh Castle 20, 70, 71, 77, 102, 103
Edmund 92
Edward I 85
Edward II of England 31
Edward Prince of Wales 105, 112
Eilean Donan Castle 34, 35, 36
Eilean Tioram (the dry island) 25

Emchath 33
English-Scottish 112
English Crown Jewels 102
English Warden of Scotland 105
Errol 92
Erskine 58
Erksine, John - 24th Earl of Mar 60

F

Falkland Palace 75, 76
Farquharson 58
Feudalism 17
Firth of Clyde 8, 16, 18, 64, 125
Firth of Forth 8, 64, 76, 95, 111, 113, 114, 115
Fleming, Sir Malcolm 69
Flodden Hill 92
Florida 41, 42
Forbes 56, 57, 80
Forbes, William 57
Forest of Mar 59
Fotheringhay Castle 113
Franco-Scottish alliance 112
Fraser 50, 83, 85, 86
Fraser, Sir Simon 84, 85, 86
Fyvie Castle 80, 81, 82

G

Galloway 119
Glamis Castle 107, 108, 109, 110
Glasgow 15, 85
Glenerochty 30
Glenluce Abby 88
Glen Mor 28
Glen Tilt 38
Glorious Revolution of 1688 50
Gordon 12, 22, 32, 68, 80
Gordon, George - Marquis of Huntly 23

Graham 97
Grant 32
Great Forest of Caledon 59
Greyfriars Kirk 30
Guardian of Scotland 85
Gueldres, Mary 48
Guise, Mary de 75, 77

H

Haakon 17
Haakon's son 17
Haakon IV of Norway 17
Hadrian's Wall 8, 64
Haliwick 78
Hallbar Tower 118, 119
Halliday 104
Hampton Court Palace 112
Hanoverian 25, 125
Harie Stewart of Gogar 119
Hay 83
Hebrides Islands 14
Henreitte Stewart, Marquis of Huntly 23
Henry VIII 105, 112
Hepburn 97
Hermitage Castle 97, 98, 100
Herries 104
Highlands 7, 8
Highland Boundary Line 8
Highland Games 60
Highland Society 61
Hoddom Castle 104, 105, 106
Holyrood Abbey 77
Holy Bible 108
Honours of Scotland 102, 103
Horace 7
Horseman of Mull 28
Howard 92
Hume (Home) 91, 92
Hume Castle 91, 92, 93
Huntly 23, 92
Huntly Castle 22, 23

I

Inchcolm Abbey 96
Inchcolm Island 95, 96
Ireland 6, 8, 20, 26, 33, 131, 132
Irish Sea 8
Irvines 104
Island of Donan 35
Isle of Arran 17
Isle of Barra 13, 14, 15
Isle of Bute 16, 17, 18
Isle of Canna 41
Isle of Cumbraes 17
Isle of Eigg 41
Isle of Iona 33
Isle of Lismore 53
Isle of Man 30, 125
Isle of Muck 41
Isle of Mull 27, 41
Isle of Rum 41
Isle of Skye 14

J

Jacobite 15, 21, 23, 25, 28, 31, 33, 34, 42, 45, 48, 50, 52, 53, 55, 58, 62, 77, 78, 81, 82, 103, 125, 131, 138
Jacobite Uprisings 81
James 71
James II 69, 71
James III 48
James IV 48, 92
James V 75, 76, 77, 112
James VI 50, 119
James VI & I 106
Jester 47, 48, 131
John, Master of Maxwell 105

K

Keith 78, 101
Kennedy 87, 124, 125
Kennedy, Archibald 125
Kennedy, David 126
Kennedy, Gilbert 88, 90

Kennedy, Quinton 90
Kennedy, Sir Thomas - 9th Earl of Cassillis 126
Kenneth's Hill 59
Keppoch Castle 39
Kilchurn Castle 54, 55
Kilravock Castle 49, 50, 51
Kindrochit 60
Kindrochit Castle 60
Kingdom of Dalriada 8
Kingdom of England 86
Kingdom of Man 17
Kingdom of Northumbria 64
Kingdom of Scotland 8, 21, 64, 84, 92, 105
King Alexander I 95
King Alexander III 17
King Consort of Scotland 106
King Edgar of Scotland 17
King Edward 20
King Edward I 85
King Edward II of England 30
King Haakon 17
King Henry IV 126
King Henry VII 76
King Henry VIII 105, 106
King James II 48, 70
King James IV 92
King James V 75, 76, 112, 119
King John Balliol 85
King Magnus 17
King Magnus III of Norway 17
King William I's 17
Kinniff Kirk 103
Kintyre Peninsula 17
Kirkudbright 72
Kirkwall 17
Kirk of St. Fergus 109
Kisimul Castle 12, 13, 14, 15

L

Laird Maxwell 105
Legend 7
Lennox 92
Liddel River 98
Lindsay 78, 80, 101, 116
Linlithgow 76
Linlithgow Palace 74, 75, 77
Little Minch 13
Livingston 70, 71, 72
Lochmaben 76
Loch Awe 54, 55
Loch Duich 35
Loch Laich 52
Loch Ness 33
Loch Ness Monster 33
Loch of Moidart 25
Loch Rannoch 30
Loch Shiel 25
Loch Spynie 117
Loch Sunart 25
Lockhart 118
London, England 86, 112
Longshanks 85
Lords of Parliament 92
Lord Admiral 92
Lord Darnley 106
Lord Dunure, the 4th Earl of Cassilis 88
Lord Herries 106
Lord Lyon King of Arms 25
Lord Maitland 119
Lord Methven 112
Lord of Badenoch 85
Lord of Man 125
Lord Protector of England 102
Lord Wharton 105, 106
Lowlands 7, 8, 64, 105
Lunquard 38
Lyon 107
Lyon, Margaret 90

M

MacAlpine, Kenneth 8
MacDonald 24, 25, 31, 32, 33, 36, 38, 40, 41, 42, 90
MacDonalds at Mingary 41
Macdonald of Clanranald 24, 25
MacDonald of Keppoch 38
MacDougall 29, 30, 31, 42
MacDougall, Alexander 30
MacDougall, John - Lorne 30
MacDougall Chief 30
MacDuff 22
MacGregor 54
MacIan 40
Mackenzie 34, 36
Mackenzie, Sir John - Coul 50
Maclean 26, 27, 28, 41, 42, 44
Maclean, Ewan 27
Macleans of Duart 27
Macleans of Lochbuie 27
Maclennar 36
Macleod 43, 44, 45
MacNeil 12, 13, 15
Macrae 34
Madeleine of Valois 75, 77
Mad Earls Walk 108
Magnus 17
Maitland 78, 118
Malcolm Canmore 60
Manxmen 125, 126
Margaret of Denmark 48
Massacre of Glencoe 48
Maxwell 68, 105, 106
Maxwell, John 105
Meldrum 80
Melrose Abbey 81
Methven 30, 112
Mingary Castle 40, 41, 42
Minister of Moneydie 102
Monster of Glamis 108
Montgomery 120, 121
Montrose 92
Moot Hill 20
Moray Valley 117
Mortimer 56, 57, 94
Mortimer, William de 95
Mortimers Deep 96
Morvin 53
Murray 19, 78, 85, 104
Murray, Andrew 85
Murray of Atholl 37

N

Neidpath Castle 83
Nine Stone Rig 98
Normans 64, 130
Norseman 17
Northern Ireland 8
Northumberland 119
North Sea 8, 64, 102
Norway 16, 17, 18, 130
Norwegian 17, 18

O

Oban 15, 30
Orkney Islands 17

P

Parish of St. Andrew 60
Pass of Brander 30
Peebleshire 84, 85
Perth 20, 85
Perthshire hills 30
Peterborough Cathedral 113
Pictish 33
Pictish King 60
Picti – Painted Ones 33
Picts 8, 33
Pipers Brae 125
Pipers Hill 92
Pope John XXII 86
Preston 80
Protestant Reformation 88

Q

Queen Elizabeth 41, 112

R

Randolph, Thomas - Earl of Moray 36
Rannoch Moor 30
Redcap 6, 99, 100, 132

Regent of Scotland 77
Reivers 119
Repentance Tower 106
River Awe 30
River Clunie 60
River Esk 53, 105
River Nairn 50
River Ness 33
River Thames 84
River Tieth 47
River Tweed 79, 83
River Ythen 82
Robert II 18
Robert III 18
Rock of the Cormorants 52
Rose 49, 50
Rose, Elizabeth - the 25th Baroness 51
Roslin 85
Rothesay 17
Rothesay Castle 16, 17, 18
Rough Wooing 106
Roxburgh 48
Running Trade 125
Ruthven 19

S

Sadler. Sir Ralph 112, 113
Scone Palace 19, 20, 21, 30, 102, 103
Scott 97
Scottish Nationalists 20
Scottish Parliament 50
Scottish Wars of Independence 84
Sea raven 117
Sennachies 6, 38
Seton 22, 80
Sharp 104
Sheffield 113
Shetland Islands 17
Soulis, William de 98
Southern Islands 17
Southern Uplands 64

Spaniards 41
Spanish Armada 41
Spynie Palace 116, 117
St. Andrew 48, 59, 60
St. Andrew's Cross 48
St. Andrews 30, 62, 85
St. Columba 33, 50, 95
St. Fergus 109, 110
St. Fergus's Cave 110
St. Fergus Kirk 108, 109
St. Margaret 72, 85
St. Margaret's Chapel 72
St. Mary's Church in Hertfordshire 113
St. Matthew 106
St. Pierre de Riems, France 77
St. Rule or Regulas 59, 60
Stalker Castle - see Castle Stalker
Stanley, Sir John 126
Stewart 16, 17, 23, 31, 33, 37, 46, 47, 48, 52, 74, 76, 77, 78, 79, 90, 97, 113, 117, 118, 119, 129, 132, 138
Stewart, Alexander 17, 53
Stewart, James - Duke of Rothesay 76
Stewart, Robert - 1st Duke of Albany 47
Stewart, Robert - Duke of Albany 76
Stewarts of Appin 53
Stewart chief, Duncan, 7th 53
Stewart (Stuart) 74
Stewart – Dukes of Albany 46
Stewart of Ahtoll 37
Stewart of Appin 52
Stewart of Buchan 78
Stirling 47, 85, 95
Stirling Bridge 85
Stone of Destiny 20, 21
Stone of Scone 20
Strathbogie 23

Stuart 125
Stuart, Charles Edward 79
Stuart, James Francis Edward - The Old Pretender 25
Stuart, Mary - Queen of Scots 38, 39, 50, 76, 77, 78, 86, 90, 93, 103, 105, 106, 112, 113, 115, 117
Sudreys - Southern Islands 17
Surrey 92

T

Tantallon Castle 111, 112
The Mad Earl 108
Thirlestane Castle 119
Thomas the Rymer 81
Threave Castle 5, 68, 69, 72, 73, 129
Tioram Castle - see Castle Tioram
Tobermory Bay 41
Tower of London 84
Traquair House 78
Treaty of Berwick 86
Treaty of Edinburgh-Northampton 86
Treaty of Norham 106
Treaty of Perth 17
True Thomas 81
Tudor, Margaret 48, 112
Tyndrum 30

U

Union of the Crowns 81
Urquhart Castle 32, 33
Uspak 17
Uspak as King of Man and the Isles 17

V

Village of Doldencha 59
Vipont 114

W

Wallace, Sir Malcolm 85
Wallace, Sir William 84, 85, 86, 103
Wars of Scottish Independence 17, 85
Watson 78, 94
Wemyss 83
Western Isles 17
Westminster 30
Westminster Abbey 20, 113
Wharton 106
Wherry 53
Wingfield 113

Y

York 76

By the Same Author:

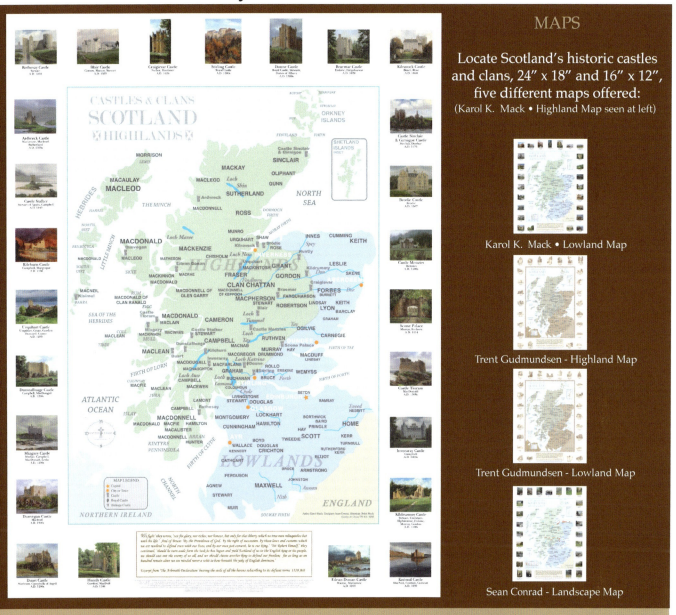

MAPS

Locate Scotland's historic castles and clans, 24" x 18" and 16" x 12", five different maps offered:
(Karol K. Mack • Highland Map seen at left)

Karol K. Mack • Lowland Map

Trent Gudmundsen - Highland Map

Trent Gudmundsen - Lowland Map

Sean Conrad - Landscape Map

OVER 100 NEW SCOTTISH PRODUCTS AT: WWW.CASTLESANDCLANS.COM
BOOK • MAPS • PRINTS • HISTORICAL TIMELINE

ALSO AVAILABLE

PRINTS: Over one hundred castles and landscapes available - sizes vary. Giclee on canvas reproduction on paper. 11" x 17" total size, framed size is 11" x 14".

TIMELINE: Explore Scotland's history in a visual format. 24" x 36" and 23" x 35". From 3500 B.C. to A.D. 2000.

VISIT OUR WEBSITE
WWW.CASTLESANDCLANS.COM

OR CALL TO ORDER
970.577.9627

LOCH VALE FINE ART™
EST. 2000

ESTES PARK, CO
U.S.A. 80517

OVER 100 NEW SCOTTISH PRODUCTS AT: WWW.CASTLESANDCLANS.COM
BOOK • MAPS • PRINTS • HISTORICAL TIMELINE

Printed in Great Britain
by Amazon

34957920R00082